THE MOUNTAIN

A Journey in Time, Truth, and Love

James S. Sherman

Formatting by Daniel J. Mawhinney

www.40DayPublishing.com

Cover design by Jonna Feavel

www.40DayGraphics.com

Printed in the United States of America

Table of Contents

A Word from the Author

Troubled by the sound of the thunder, and the sudden brightness of lightening, the storm, while distinct seemed to be next. Why was this so real, at a time when other things seemed to be less than important?

Then, the flash of lightening stopped and the sound disappeared for a moment because I heard the sound of Love in the distance of time, and perhaps wanting to hear more, I felt like she was standing very close to me. Why was that so much a part of now?

Thinking I called for her: Love, Love? Where are you? Then the silence. What was it I heard? Was it her, or was it my imagination, or my need? That was strange because it sounded so close. Perhaps wanting to go back toward the mountain, and perhaps looking where I first found her was the process or the perfect place for my next steps. Why? Then I saw the lightening again, and heard the sound almost immediately of thunder within the range of where I was. A warning? Perhaps or then it could just be that I was on the outside of not knowing reality.

Stepping toward the base of the mountain was the necessary task. Each step closer than the last, and each step more important than one of the others. Now the sound I wanted to hear again was the sound of Love barking to me or toward me, knowing that I would come and find her. She is also known now to me as Encephalitis.

Encephalitis or inflammation of the brain tissue, is rare, affecting about one in 200,000 people each year in the U.S. When it strikes, it can be very serious, causing personality changes, seizures, weakness, and other symptoms depending on the part of the brain affected. (Web MD).

This was the medical term and diagnosis of the issue. From approximately early 2008 until now the process has been completed. From initial diagnosis with medical surgery on the left side of my brain area to being released and sent home to "finish" what the medical team could not or would not document.

Introduction

Welcome to the world of non-existence thinking about something, someone, or some place that may become the distant future of time. Time as a four letter word is perhaps the reason for existence for anything, at any moment and yet when something or someone suddenly comes to exist the reason, or gaining process is only to be measured in steps of acceptance. So what time is it?

TIME (T) could be for treasure, while (I) could be for Imagine, and then (M) would have meaning, while (E) might remain examine.

That perhaps makes The Truth different to deal with:

Examination of the concept of truth is very interesting. There is a scripture that states we shall know the truth and the truth will set us free. John 8:32.

T-TIME OF TREASURE

R-REASON OF IMAGINATION

U-UNITY IN UNDERSTANDING

T-TESTING VISIBILITY OF TIME

H-HOPEFULL OF TIME, TRUTH, AND

LOVE

Now that time and truth have been responded to. What about Love.

Love is certainly within a period of life also known as time. Love is the third item, in the content document.

Now then looking at LOVE:

(L) with the length of itself measurable, to (o) which is observation of length, and of course–(V) visible observation of length and (E) for everlasting observation.

The Mountain

In The Beginning, driving west, suddenly, for a specific reason I noticed the mountain. As if it were a magnet, it seemed to say, "Come to Me." Without speeding, I kept thinking why? There was a distance between the mountain and I and there was a reason why the spirit of movement towards it was such a demanding force. The movement was necessary. The movement was peaceful, demanding, and special.

Troubled by the emotion, concerned for the lack of understanding, and confused by the distance to the next place of safety. Yes, it was at the base of the mountain, that strangely, my attention was captured.

Does this place, this mountain, have a name? There are many different things or reasons. The fact is, the mountain is where I am and the need to climb higher appears in front of me without understanding. Unsure of why, or where, the day seems cool, yet comfortable. The location, quiet but safe, and the place secure around me. Why Not? Move upward for a time and see what is ahead? When it is time to rest, or wonder, the day is still quite early, and the angle of climb seems not to be difficult at least for the moment, perhaps a little higher up, and sight of some distant place will be visible.

Climb then, for a while and see if the reason for being away from the past and the problem is worth living for, yet, worth leaving for a time to climb on the mountain. There seems to be a path to follow around the rock, close to the edge of this difficult area, and yet the path seems to have been placed there to follow.

Even the sound of my steps were noticeable. The breaking of the little limbs, the crunch of leaves and movement of stone beneath my steps. Why had I not noticed that before? What was the sound or did I mistake something for lack of reason? Oh, there in the hollow of the valley below is a deer, and it looks like, yes it is a family of them moving quietly, yet securely, along the path that I had just walked.

Perhaps, resting here would not be such a bad idea, especially since there seems to be so much more to look at. Off to the east, the distance of space seems to excite me. How to go that far? Simply enough, look to the west and wonder about the steep climb in wall of rock that appears so close and yet so far. Why do I wonder about how it got that way? What should be the name of something that beautiful? Oh now I know, that could be called "tomorrow." It is not reachable today and does not look like it will be gone for a while.

Looking down is uncomfortable, because something inside makes me feel that is something that should not be done. That something makes me, pushes me, to look up instead to a place that is visible and yet demands more of me, to move forward within my desire at the presence of time and is the concern for not standing still.

The mountain, then, is here and I am with it, yet I am able to continue to move from a place that seems to be a place to be left behind, and move to a place that seems to be somewhere up and beyond any place that I have been before. The sun, the breeze and the wild life around seems to be a magnitude of visibility. Secure in where I am, yet wanting to climb higher and soon, to be someplace that is perhaps more exciting than where I was when I started to climb the mountain.

The clouds seem to be closer to me than when I started, and the blue of the sky seems to be more touchable, or visibility of it seems to be more enjoyable. Why? Yes, I am higher than I was earlier in the day. The look seems so far from where I am and the time placing me here seems to be noticeable. The weather is still very enjoyable as the path on the mountain seems to be greatly improved and more clearly visible. Even the sound of the wild life has gotten stronger and the life all around seems to be closer to me than when I started this climb.

The mountain is part of me, the mountain is a place where I can be, and is strongly a place of protection and comfort. The mountain is mine and I will continue to climb.

Oh yes, time has arrived and in some way, the storm was remembering again. Part of the past that was lost because I had begun to climb a mountain.

There is a measurement in space of place that we call time. We ask about it almost without thinking why. We say "What time is it?" Yet seemingly it must be something important or we would be silly to ask. The message of the past has to start someplace in time, for me it is a remembered age of three. Perhaps part of that will come forward in this mountain. Perhaps not because it was difficult to think back at, and more difficult to remember now that it was very close to something in me, also known as the time of childhood. What a reason to climb up?

Half Up or Half Down

Returning to the look ahead, I noticed a very tall and beautiful green tree, which seemed to be saying "come to me." Walking over I noticed that not only was it very strong, visible from a distance, but even more powerfully magnetic as I got closer to it. Immediately it was if the tree was speaking to me. "Touch my limbs", "Know That I Am Here."

Pondering the reasoning behind, or in front of this tall and greatly beautiful place, there was a movement of the wind, and one limb seem to move quickly towards the west, and there exposed was another pathway, leading slightly down, and away from the tree. Powerfully wanting to be walked, and drawing me even quicker around the tall and beautiful green tree, into a new place.

Knowing that I was close to being half way up the mountain, and moving from a fixed location of half way to start down the mountain I was excited about going even quicker into a wider pathway toward what looked like a place of pleasure, and a valley of beauty. Knowing that time was still on my side, and not being concerned about the setting sun, I walked even faster toward the sound of running water. There behind, slightly hidden by another large tree, was a beautiful water fall and the sound of a voice from the mountain saying, "Thank you for being with me."

What a perfect place to spend the evening and, for a first visit, look at the immediate beauty of something almost beyond description. Already, it seemed like it was pulling me into a relationship of wanting to be there forever, yet, for some reason, I remembered that I was half way up a mountain, or so I thought.

Resting for the night, I found some mint and some other green that appealed to my desire to have love, and the night quickly set into another form of beauty. As the sun set, the wind laid down, and the birds began to enter into rest, I, noticeable as it was, saw the moon rise in a different way. So clear, so full, and so large. Why had I never seen it so beautifully there before?

As I settled down for rest, the sound of the waterfall seemed to be singing a night time melody of peace, love, and presence for a force that was beyond any description. Then, I fell into a peaceful, needful rest and seemed to have settled. Even though I was not at the top of the mountain, I did not need or desire to go down from this place of peaceful rest.

Midway between the two measurable places of time, I awoke with the sound of an aircraft flying very high overhead. Not to supplement, but a reminder, that being in between the top and bottom of this mountain, I was also in between staying down and getting up. Should I continue to explore the valley or go back to the big tall tree and climb higher? Quickly, yet with some regret I, turned back toward the place and point of time that had caused me to be in this special place.

How high up would I go to reach the stopping place of this mountain? Not in fear, but in a strong possibility of failure or resentment, I returned to the entrance point of the beautiful and powerful place of peace. Now, the decision was to go higher? Wondering about why, or how, that would measure later in life, if it truly would be something to remember, was a motivation that quickened my thinking when I reached the turning point. Now the excitement of climbing towards a future of wonder begins. With determination, thankfulness, and reminiscence, expectations will surpass imagination

What's above, could be more powerfully wonderful than the camp site for the night? The sound of the birds, my heart with a light and wondering purpose. Noticeably life changes were all around. The size and color of the rocks and the path that I walked on seemed, in some ways, to narrow.

The climb to a higher location was an interesting place, because, perhaps, I noticed a change in my walk, and a change in my thinking. Higher? Why? When would high enough be visible? Suddenly the urge to turn around and start down became overwhelming. Pause, wait, listen and think? No, that was not the right choice. The word "prayer" came suddenly into my thinking process.

Why pray, and for what? I was alone in the place some would call God's creation, and in the place of time alone, with a peace of mind, that seemed to want to be in me. Then I noticed a pair of birds very much higher, drifting in the wind and I wondered. How did they know I was there, or did they know? Did it matter that I was higher than I use to be?

The next stopping point was at a joint in the path that was a place that was distinctly evident. Left or Right? Which would I take? Why should I be concerned about one or the other? Going back to the evening before, with the large tree visible I stopped and actually said: "which way"?

The Path Around

Nearing what seemed to be the top of the mountain, which ended up to be an area level and several miles across, I stood in amazement searching for an easy answer to a difficult question. Which way to turn? Left or right, straight ahead? Each was a reasonable choice, yet, within terms of visibility, they all seemed to be unreasonable. Very easy to understand that I was not going to go down, or turn back, at this point in my life.

Looking at the ground I noticed a stone that was somewhat like an arrow head. Picking it up and thinking about it, I decided which end of the stone to use as a tool and threw it up in the air, looking for it when it landed. It pointed to the western area. The choice was made to go that way in life. Any step taken, regardless of the time of day, or the direction, is in fact noticeable if the wind is blowing. Making a choice for which path to walk should not always be difficult.

Looking down once again, I noticed a thin, but beautiful stone, which was shaped somewhat like a heart. Holding it and touching it, I wondered why? Why did I notice a stone, which looked so much like the human heart?

The wind was stronger today, than the day before, and it seemed to have purpose. Most of which seemed to be to keep the two birds I had noticed before invisible to me. They were still somewhere, but not within sight. That took me to a different holding pattern and I wondered about why I could not find peace of mind in the walk, or the path that I was taking.

Now where should I be? The path seemed to be, if I were noticeable to someone, going down towards the lower end, yet I wondered. I was on a different side, when I started the climb. The sun was telling me I headed west, even though the mountain, was telling me that I was on my way down, instead of on my way up.

Enough. Continuation was the secret, wind or no wind, clouds or no clouds, the sun was present and I was in charge of my walk once again.

Yes, I was walking down the side that seemed to invite me to continuation.

Then, as if I were looking into a mirror, I looked across the valley and saw the other side. I truly had changed sides of the mountain, but from this view point, I looked at myself and said that even that view placed me within reach of myself.

Now more than ever, I wanted to continue toward a destination. Reasonable as it was, I did not have an actual plan for going any way. My life, troubled by the past, and definitely unsettled towards the future, was right there in front of me looking around at the world, and seeing myself as stuck. Perhaps it was time, perhaps the word or the idea of prayer was noticeable again. How or why is still something to wonder about. But, I was on a path. I had climbed to the near top of a very beautiful mountain, and slept in a quiet place or valley and still was able to know that the very breath that was with me was special.

Once again, it did not seem to matter about up or down, east or west, but what did matter was the awareness of not being alone, but being nearer to something, within, or without proof, the presence of force was all around and yet not bothersome. It was touching me.

Once again I came into view of a special place. As I turned toward the wall close to the edge of the area, I noticed slightly ahead what seemed to be significantly further down a place that one might call peace. I knew that I needed to go there. Suddenly the two birds that I had seen the day before were floating high above, at peace with the wind, but over me as if to say "you're on the right path again."

Looking ahead, and looking to the left and right, I noticed that some things looked exactly the same, yet amazingly, some of the same things looked as if I were sent to touch them, feel them, or perhaps name them so that others could or would know.

Today was the day of a holiday weekend and I knew for a fact that I must start down toward home. My thinking was that going back to work would be uneventful, and it was the same as any other day except for the holiday required time off.

That also seemed like something that was totally unexpected, yet wanted because, as we had been so often told "time is money." That seemed so simply stupid in a building that had eight wings separated by doors, people, and security cards. Wanting to go back to work was not high on the list of things to do, but there was some indication that I would have to go back down to get there. Down to get where? Work, or a place that was necessarily unlocked, but still there.

What would tomorrow be like? Why should I even care about it? When I was on the road, it did not seem to matter. When I ran low on funds it did. The past days off and the thought of returning to work were both dealt with differently. I did want to stay higher on the mountain. Parts of me did not want to return or climb down. But, I must walk continually to arrive down and be in place for Tuesday.

The Friend Found

On the way down, the weather seemed to want to change. The wind was stronger, the clouds deeper and darker, and the sun seemed to want to say "I am going away." Why then did I wonder about the sound of the bark that I heard? It was distant, yet when the wind shifted it seemed to be close. It was a dog that sounded like it was near and also like it was wounded. Why?

I kept walking toward the sound as I rounded the next bunch of brushes and trees. There in the corner of a pile of rock, was a dog, shifting and pulling its right leg, seemingly stuck and in a way, hurt.

Approaching the animal, I held my right hand face down, palm extended, and spoke in a soft voice. I could not tell right away, because both the wind and the darkness had a strong hold on the problem.

Looking for a way to be safe, yet feeling a strong pull to help this animal, I could not help but wonder how the dog got here. Why was it here? Why did this have to be part of my walk? Now left, right, or straight ahead did seem to matter. The wind pushed stronger and the first clap of thunder roared loudly in my ears. I spoke to the dog, saying softly, "I'm here to help. What do you need? What can I do for you?"

For whatever the reason the dog settled down and seemed to ask for help. I noticed that the right front foot seemed to be wedged between two rocks. Slowly, softly, I touched the leg, moving my hand down to the foot, speaking in a gentle voice. "I Love You." The foot, was being restricted by the paw that was being wedged between the two rocks. Picking one, I moved it and suddenly the dog walked close to me as the rain started and the lightening became stronger and closer.

I leaned back into the rock wall and for whatever reason started humming a soft song of "love."

Then I noticed that the dog was a female and was very thin. I reached into a pocket and found some of the jerky that, for some reason, I had been keeping and gave her a piece while speaking softly to her. She moved even closer to me and we settled down in the storm, getting wet, yet feeling quiet peaceful that I was with her. The paw had been free from the rocks and a large thorn had been removed. Peaceful and quiet, she seemed to want to rest.

What was her name? How would I call her and why did I want her on the mountain with me in a journey that even I did not know why I was on? The word "love" came to mind and I stroked her, and said "Love. Love. Love."

The rain stopped, the lightening seemed to disappear, and the wind went quiet. It seemed like I was at peace and it seemed very evident that I had Love in my lap.

Now, the mountain, the direction of my walk, and the next step seemed to have more meaning for tomorrow. Why? Because I had "Love" in my hands, and she seemed to strongly want for me, to know that she was secure and pleasantly mine.

For whatever reason, it seemed like the last day of a week, or perhaps an even stronger feeling—the last day of a month—or year. Love was with me, the weather had returned to wonderful and the night sky was clearly visible as the stars began to speak again.

Saying "walk with us" and be with Love in us, for we are the direction of your desire. Such a powerful feeling, without any need for further direction, or wonder, I rested in peace the rest of the night. Waking early, Love seemed eager to move on. Now near the bottom and close to home.

Partly dreaming, or thinking safely in this place was easier than I ever remembered before. Love with me and the softness of the night was also being amplified by some other presence of peace. Within me or present outside, I noticed a star, by itself, seemingly saying "I am special." Yet I did not know why I heard that.

I wondered why a strange dog would create within me a change that was so strong. There is something in the sound of the bark—or the touch—perhaps the look— when the dog stops and just looks to see what you will do next. There is a bridge between people and pets, which needs to be examined in a way that explains the touch of each to the other. In the case of Love, she had a way of making sure you knew that she was present and that you were important to her. The rest of it was amazement because each time I looked at her there was something new, or pleasant that was not there the moment before. A different form of Time, Truth and Love in ways that needed to be documented.

Drifting into a deeper sleep I did dream that night of peacefully wanting to be somewhere permanent and knowing peace. Not necessarily over a known position, but a position that seemingly was within reach. Why, when, and where would the next change become reality? Having a new friend, being at peace with her, and having her seem to be within peace with me, made climbing the mountain on the three-day weekend well worth the time. If for no other reason she—Love—was there.

Turn Around

Beginning somewhere would be a great idea, if you knew for certain where somewhere is. Not that it makes a difference, but it is a beginning part of life.

Now, then, having opened the bottle of stuff, into a place of existences, what should, or could be next?

That thought may come again and again, but at least, it is part of what I can remember. For example: music, especially music you like has parts or sounds that you remember. The beginning, or the end, the part in-between, but you can hum that part at times.

Wanting to know more about the path I was on and why, I expected it to go in the direction of life, I needed such a moment. Now, Love seemed to know what I needed, and kept just ahead, but kept looking back to see if I was close to her.

With amazement, I wondered why she acted as if she knew every step I was going to take. To the left or right, she moved as if to guide me and then looked to see if I was following.

The pathway seemed more truthful, in the fact that it was obvious that this side of the mountain was a path that led downward. But, not to think less than the truth, down to what? Down to where? Would I need to know more?

Wondering about that, or if, or when next might appear is a good place to start. Love seemed to know and barked at me. What was interesting to the time or place? Then, the idea of something else, in a different format came into existence and it was called or started out with the name of "The Pond" and ended with the name of "The Storm."

It was to say, some force was writing in my head, the desire to know and then place that idea on paper. Like painting a picture, while listening to a great piece of music. Wanting to express what I was thinking, and also wanting Love to understand that it was her that helped me know it.

Never the less, I transferred into the concept of wanting to write, but not for sure knowing if I was to be an author. Then it hit me.

Either the first The Pond or the second The Storm, combine them into one, or start over again and see where the strange land takes me— or could that be writing?

Calling at Love, I said "heel" and it was if she knew exactly what to do. She stopped and came back to me and stood, waiting. Waiting for me to take the next step.

The walk down this path was one of interest. The concept of knowing that I wanted to write and knowing that it would be a walk up and down a path was now very present.

For some reason writing was very visible, yet it was distant in my understandable way. Not totally insecure, but not strong or controlling my movement. There must be something else between the then and the now of writing, because for the most part the only process I had completed was what is called an auto-biography document from as far back as I could remember and it is not yet readable or completed.

Walking along with Love seemed to make me willing to think differently. The influence of this animal was amazing. She stopped when I did, seem to listen for things that were of interest, and yet stepped forward as soon as I did. Where did she learn to be so in touch with reality? Why did I even wonder?

It seemed like I was going back to the first or second concept of my writing or wanting to write.

A Decision Needed

In the beginning, there was a period of doubt, being ashamed of time, and wondering about the possibility of a meaning for the future. Each day, different, than the day before and always wondering if time would make a change that could be understood.

Wondering in the past, or thinking of the future, what would indeed be a place of beginning.

That walk up the mountain had only been for a short period of three days, trying to clear my head of the difficulty that seem to lodge there. Now Love and I were at the beginning point of the climb, the mountain was there, but she and I were here. Which way should I turn?

Going back to the house, changing clothes, feeding Love and resting, I checked the mail and watched the news. All of that, except for having a dog, was what I had left the loft for. I had to go and find a climbing away point in life, something to do, yet not knowing how to do it. That might have been the core of wanting to write, without knowing the title for the book, or, the style of writing.

Having visited books stores, I could find nothing that excited me. Having written a document called "The

Pond" I was stuck in the rut of life and wanting only to find peace. Then the struggle to find peace, led to finding a dog. Now Love was part of both life and the struggle.

Then, a decision could be made. Go back to work. Call the shelter and find a home for Love. Quit my job, and climb the mountain. At least it was within walking distance of the house, and close enough to climb on one side, and come down the other.

Perhaps I had a misguided thought, but, at that moment I was not going to give up Love and I wanted to take a leave of absence from the job, which was in many ways boring. Like watching the water fall the night of my climb. I could hear it and I could see it, yet for some reason the waterfall needed more work and a deeper view for completion.

Leaving the local existing area of work, I wondered about the distance to the next destination. Within me is a desire to stay located in one place, yet also a strong desire to move away from where I am standing. Because the storm is coming and it will be impacting not only my life, but many other people that I do not even know. What time is it? Early morning? Or near lunch? Does it matter when the distance to the next step is a step in the process of getting ready for the walk that will always be remembered? The next step will be one that could be thought of in the future and seen in the past, yet it will be remembered because someone mentioned the storm.

Without knowing why, or perhaps when it seemed as if I knew change was visible or noticeable all around. Love in my life was factual but was it a blessing or was it a reasonable understanding for the need of knowledge?

When she stopped and looked up it was if she knew I needed help, and as if she could do it if I would bark. Then it was the amazing settled feeling she seemed to have when laying close to me at night. There was a relationship that was part dog, and part human. Why?

It seemed to me that time was important, yet could be understood with Love was part of time's presence. Then I wondered if she would be jealous if I had a house and a backyard?

Why would I even wonder about that? At the job, I had a silly job of placing the same size box on the shipping line, every 20 minutes and waiting for the blower to put some stupid packing into the bottom. Then it moved beyond my reach. What a way to look to tomorrow.

What Time Is It?

Pause, think it through, wonder why, but know for sure that the distance between time and the next thing is possibly shorter, but hopefully longer. Cold weather tonight, sleeping in a little longer in the morning, all of which will be better than wondering. Can it be that there is an answer to the total question of time? Wondering why I even started this job with a place called "The Mountain?"

Will the necessity of a known answer to that excuse, the need for explanation, or why the cloud is so strong in my vision at the present time be visible in an answer to my questions?

The distance between start and completion is measurable. When I let Love back in the house, I noticed that she was asking for something else. Perhaps today was the day I should make a decision as to the amount of time that I have available and what should be done with that time. Writing?

Then the conflict of time, reason, and of course, income for living, all are part of the path. That was partly why I reasoned while on the job here working in the mountain. The trip was for a reason, perhaps desperation, and yet, finding Love and acting on that foundation turned my climb a different direction.

Wondering about all the process of having a reason for writing, or a reason for petting the dog, both being something to do, are interesting conflicts of time that seem somewhat difficult to manage.

Looking back at the content of "My Life," which is not published yet needed to be available, is a strange way of wondering. Distance from the past, and keeping up with the current process is done in "The pond." Both are different and yet they are both the same. A process of time in need of a process for existence.

What time is it? When someone asks is it now, or is it then, depending on the tone of voice they use, I will help it be tomorrow for them, so that the hurt of hearing is being aided. It is time to begin, and it is time to stay away, and it is time for a reason to write. Perhaps then the name of the book to be written is the problem of progression.

It was easy to give Love her name because of the circumstance with which she came into my life. Letting her become something that I need. She is Love and I need Love to be me and in me.

Before you sit your clock back, because of a time zone change, in higher life or drive, remember that the time you left was the time you had before you changed your clock. The same though would be for setting your watch ahead in the spring of your life. Truly, do we know what time it is?

Struggling with time is an option, however, if you're employed. Your time starts and stops by a clock that you have little control over. Think about why, or when, but remember the clock is ticking always against what you might like to know. Remembering it took two hours to get the job, and I knew I could quiet or lose it in minutes, I was always thinking about tick and tock: the clock.

The inside effort of Monday through Friday, with an occasional overtime Saturday, is part of life, but the struggle is trying to remember that there was a beginning. Perhaps there is also the reluctant concept of not dealing with the end. Who, in their working normal mind, would wonder about stuff like that? The time that I had, was set because of a need. The stop I made here at the mountain, because from a distance the mountain seemed to be there, was necessary for me to see. Time.

The day, was at an end, with the sun about to set, and I was hungry, and there was a sign on the side of the road, saying "help wanted." Right next to the sign was another sign saying "food." What more could a necessary empty with nothing person need to do to stop and rest?

Some reason the tomorrow did not seem to matter and the mountain was so close that it seemed to have a sign itself and saying "come climb." What an invitation.

Knowing and accepting Love as part of life, would have to be a discussion with her. Wanting to keep her, was strong, and most of all doable. That part of her was settled. Yet deep inside the question did remain. What time is it?

A New Day

Here I am, in the process of wanting to stay, yet a stronger force says, that today is a new day and it has begun. Now then, why did the sun come up? What is the very next thing to think about or remember? Suddenly Love nudged me and looked up with what appeared to be anxious activity and headed towards the door.

The mountain was out there, but did she expect me to climb? Why was she so anxious to be outside? The sun was breaking the horizon, and the wind low. The sky seemed very blue, and for some reason, I did not even remember that it was Saturday and a day off from the activity of necessity. Walking along the pathway, looking down and around I heard the sound of two birds singing.

The light all around seemed to be so peaceful and the color of the blue in the sky seemed to be so special. We were not in a hurry. There seemed to be an indefinite direction of both time and necessity. Love seemed to be anxiously pulling toward down town and it seemed as if she knew it was a special day. But how?

Looking again at my watch I noticed that it was 06:20. Six was not special as I was normally up at six and almost ready for work. The 20 stood high on my attention, and

THE MOUNTAIN

I noticed that 20 was a combination of two 10s or 4 fives. Why did I even notice that?

Love stopped at that moment and looked back at me and barked four times, each the same bark and seemed to be very aggressive at wanting to cross the street right where we were. Looking both ways I walked with her to the other side of the street and looking down, I saw a stone shaped like a heart. Picking it up, looking at it, and touching it, I wondered why my heart beat so strongly.

In the window of the business was an example of multiple ways to build a yard pond. I had a definite remembrance that I had no yard to speak of. Building a yard pond was definitely not something I had wanted to do, yet it seemed to stay in my thought process. *You do not even have a gold fish to swim in the pond that needs to be built.*

Now I knew that I needed to go back in time and rethink why, where, when, and wonder about the past, and the reason why there was no yard pond. Did it matter? Was it important? Why? The sun moved in such a way that it brightly reflected off another item in the store window.

Five or six blocks from the loft, with Love sitting quietly next to me, the wind suddenly picked up as if to tell me to move. That was easy but now I wondered about which direction the yard pond would be, or when the gold fish would be purchased, and if the gold fish had brothers and sisters. How big was the yard pond?

Love started down the walk way again. She looked back and barked. Sounded like she said "come on I do not have time to sit and do nothing." Why was she so anxious to consider moving again? We were a block away from the early morning coffee shop and she seemed to know that. Almost running she stopped at the front door, laid down, and looked up.

Yes, this was a new day. It may have been a Saturday, and it may have been a different day, but for some reason it seemed like a special day. Going in I sat at the booth I liked and ordered coffee and looked out the window at Love. She seemed perfectly at peace. I began to see the yard pond and I saw multiple gold fish, fresh fish, Koi, and the waterfall at the south end. Water moved from there to the north end over another water fall. I seemed to be at peace.

A gentleman asked if he could sit with me. Smiling largely, he asked "Is she your dog?" Looking out the window I saw Love with her tail wagging and I said "her?" He laughed. "I had a dog like her and lost her last year to a storm. She was expecting and left for some reason to climb the mountain." My heart flipped and I could not wonder why, but I ask him if his dog looked like her? What was his dog's name? He said "Love." My heart flipped and I started crying. Suddenly I felt the rock in my hand shake. I said, "Sir, I think she is your dog."

Then I shared the climb I had on the mountain that day, finding her, and helping her get free.

Beginning Again

John Masterson formerly introduced himself. He asks me in what part of the business I was employed. He said, as the retired owner of "The Mountain" his interest was still 55% of their thinking and because he was still part of the team, he watched the process very diligently.

Amazing as it was his dog, Love, was leaving my life and he as the original owner of the business I worked at, was suddenly joining it.

I had seen photos on the hallway walls but had paid little attention because I had always thought I would only work a little while before I went somewhere else in life.

John seemed to be very interested in the fact that I had climbed the mountain and the reason I had done so. He moved me into thinking about the different point that I saw as I had climbed several weeks before. What did I think? What was visible? What was the sound of what I heard and the image of what I saw? Interesting questions for a man that I had only just met.

As we talked I felt warm inside, and wondered if we'd met because of my previously powerful relationship with Love. Asking about her, he informed me that she was a gift from his wife before she had passed away, and named by his wife when she gave the dog to him. She had said that the fact remains very powerful. That even though the name "Love" was a four letter word, there was much more to the understanding. Love, explained in each of us, is visible to someone else differently. How did we see?

Now the mountain seemed to be so much more of a friend, rather than a place to run to as a place of escape. Love still watching from outside, stood and leaned against the glass window. John said, it was time to go, but he would be in contact? What did that mean?

As John left, Love seemed to be excited and jumped against him with several barks. It was as if she was saying "I am home now." But, even though I thought I knew dog talk, was I at home now? Was there another reason to climb the mountain, or should I go back to the loft and seek an answer about why the business and the mountain had the same name?

That was a path that I could walk because I had learned several things about myself. The first that seemed most important was that I did miss the dog being beside me. Calling softly and quietly, I did say "come Love."

Entering the loft I felt good inside, and sad at the same time. Something said "study" so I immediately started my lap top and went to the google search box and typed in the city name, and with a plus sign in-between the word "mountain."

The first thing I noticed was that the word mountain had eight letters. Why did I notice that? Eight—may signify, although many scholars don't attribute any symbolic meaning to this number.

This was a perfect way of thinking out loud, about who, or why, or when, for me because I was at a new beginning, yet did not know why, who I was, or when I would remember the right climb on the mountain.

Suddenly I remembered something about the day Love was in my life. I reached a point that seemed to have a choice to the "left" or "right" and I had to make a decision. Why did I choose the right path or that direction? Perhaps because I am right handed? No, not that, but something made me pick "right." I am glad the left side did not say "wrong."

Getting back to the computer screen, I noticed something else in the google search box. Many choices of information. That was wonderful, so to speak, at least I could say that I did not know which click of the mouse should be made.

But, deeper still, was the wonder or the reason why the person, whoever they are, said the things for each page? Why did they define the page or the next click of the internet that way?

There was a reason, for the path now and I knew there was a "beginning." Not to write or to pet the missing dog, but to "study."

Working Without

What's in a number? The days we were off from work or the days left until payday? What does it matter? Reading the group email information as always required looking for the next this or that. I was working without a reason, for understanding why the rest of the things I wondered about, did not pass my mind while I was climbing the mountain. Then John Masterson came into existence, just as my intercom buzzed.

The office said I should come up right away and bring a notebook. It was not staff meeting day, and it was not I forgot something day, or was it? Perhaps it would answer another question. How long would I be working here? Saying, yes sir, as I walked into the leader's office of shipping, he said sit down man, I need to talk.

Asking in a secret voice he said, "How long have you been part of the team?" "Why?" I said. "It has been a little more than six months. Is there something wrong? Is there a problem with my work load? Why am I here?" Within the moment I felt like I was about to join the unemployed.

Our branch received a call from someone who indicated that you had an interest in the 8th wing of our complex.

Shipping? What is it you are interested in? It was not so much an interest as it was a question about what and why the company said we were "do able." Did our shipping the way we do? What exactly? The rumor I heard was that there is a lot of stuffing that fills an almost empty box and it leaves the plant.

Where did you hear that? What part of the plant? It is more junk mail on the group site than fact I said. My lead said, we happy folks have been shipping in the same box for several years. Why change that?

The product we send is a visual picture of us by the customer that received the box. The first thing they see is all of the wasted filler, and what they want to see is what they are expecting. Not what filler feels like. Perhaps if the filler was more colorful, say at thanksgiving, or Christmas. Something besides a lot of stuff in a box that hides the product.

What would you do then, if welcomed to the shipping wing? When you came to work, what impressed you to be at this job? Why work here? The person who saw me at the door was the most impressive. He said, "I only have five more days, you must be my replacement."

The rest of that week was orientation, paper work and testing. More of a do this, do that, and give me this, or give me that paper stuff. Nothing personal, but I felt like an animal. Then the leader said: "Is that why John called us"?

We were told to upgrade your job title to building manager, dog qualified, and to do it today.

Your being moved to the front office. Then we were told he would talk to the board at the next controller meeting and to make sure you were there. I am the lead in this branch, and you are now working in the "front" office of "The Mountain." Please get out of my office and close the door. I am confused.

Looking over my shoulder, I said "yes sir" and also said thank you for "barking" at me. It will be fun to go to the next staff meeting. What color suit should I wear? Should I come in early that day? What time does that crew get to work?

Walking along the hallway, I noticed several people whispering and turning away. It seemed like there had been a storm of some sort and it also seemed as if the lightening had struck. Now, where was the front office? Who was the lead? What should I say?

When I walked through the door a couple of people said hello, Mr. Wonderful, how did you get a change in your job so quickly and what do we do to help you get settled in. The office here is on the sunset side of the building, and we will relocate you to the east side if you want sunrise. Welcome to "The Mountain."

Working Within

The office I was shown was different because I do not remember this part of the business from the time I was hired. Opening a door, the lady said "this is yours, I think. Let me know what you need."

Walking into the room I was amazed at its appearance. First because of the large desk, and second because of the single empty book shelf. Nearly empty—there was something on it. The window blinds were drawn shut so I opened them. Immediately I noticed the visible path or view to "The mountain." Suddenly the name of the business became very real.

Turning to the desk, I moved to the chair which seemed to be placed correctly. Moving it I immediately noticed that it had no wheels. It was a straight back heavy chair with no rollers. Why? I did not know but I needed to sit down so I did. Looking out the biggest window of my life I saw the mountain and also across the room, I saw the book shelf with a book on it.

I moved the chair back and went to the shelf. On the shelf was a bible in black. I opened the cover, and inside the first clear page were the words: "John with Love." Why was that book there? Why the bible?

Suddenly the alarm system started making a noise and I was jolted back into the now of life. The lady said, "come on, we must leave." Wondering why I followed her out the nearest exit. It was a little higher in the outside view than I remembered and I noticed the different groups of people gathering outside.

The door we came out of was labeled "administration." The rest of the doors, except one was unknown. The furthest door, which was my older location, was also known as "shipping."

I ask the lady closest to me about the others. She said "Door blue is Legal; door Back and White is sales, door with blue is contractors, and door short sleeve is networks. My question to her then was, "Why is that door eight empty?" She said door eight west is a closed wing of the building.

"Welcome to The Mountain, Mr...what is your name?" I said that I had been told I was building manager—dog qualified, but you could call me Jim."

"Thanks, Jim, we are officially on strike as of five minutes ago. I do not know what legal has called the strike for, but we will be told." Shortly a member of the all blue legal team came by and said we were on strike for higher wages and it was an informal strike that would only last 15 or 20 minutes. It was being done to illustrate the power of the legal reasons for this business.

My question now was: "what is this business if it is still called The Mountain"? Why was my office where it was at and what did it mean to say that I was now there? The next day, or the next week, or the next month was far beyond my ability to think at the moment and I wanted to go climb the mountain.

The alarm stopped ringing and we all started back into the building. I noticed that it was almost time for lunch and wondered if I could learn anything from watching the employees do their lunch break.

Some left the building, and some stayed. That was not much help. Of the office staff only the lady that talked with me outside remained behind and she seemed to just be sitting at her desk. I ask if she would like to split a sandwich with me.

Her openness was amazing, because straight up, she said "What church do you go to?" The lump in my throat could be felt and I thought that it was visible, but I said "I do not go anywhere" She said "Why?"

The communication seemed to be like it was coming from John Masterson, in a way, because of the direct straight forward approach. We shared casual information, and at five minutes to 1:00 pm she said, back to work. My last question was can you help me? She said, "That's why I am paid."

What do you want? "Come into the office and let's talk about that" was my reply. She picked up a steno pad and followed me in. Her first question was: "Do you know Mr. Masterson?"

Working Inside of Self

One in the afternoon of the first day, in a new office, in a new way, I was still employed by the same force. Yet something was different. Movement within and without the building close to the starting point of "The Mountain."

Asking my steno, her name, she said "Carol." What should I expect from you? She said you are my boss and I am your administrative assistant by title. What do you want from me? I said to her, the mountain, required loyalty to anyone who is climbing up. It requires learning to safely walk along the path and above all, the path requires your feet to be anchored on level ground. That is what I require.

The first thing tomorrow I want to have a walk through the building at 8:00 a.m. With the chief or boss of each branch of office present. We open at 9:00 a.m. The walk through will be completed by then. You, along with me too, be there. We will take an initial look at each and every location. Nothing more.

A directory of staff people and the last official documentation they sent to anyone for any reason will help. Can you do that today before closing and set up the visit with each branch for the 8:00 time.

It is close to 4:00 and when you are ready and completed you can take the rest of the day off. Take an expense card and buy a new pair of walking shoes, a new work out fit that you like, and a new recorder that will audio and video what we do tomorrow. Tomorrow will be different.

The evening office clock on the wall indicated it was officially the end of the day. I had worked for eight hours, yet felt like I had been there for two or three days. Why? Did this become something I would regret? Thinking about tomorrow, I wondered exactly what I would see behind each door and I wondered more why wing eight was empty. Why and what to do with that? I knew administration, shipping, and the bathroom doors. What else do I need to know?

Walking to the car I thought of Love and her not being at home. I wanted to go directly to the mountain and start climbing, but common sense said go back to the loft and rest. You might even pray. Pray? What was that and where did that come from?

After a quick microwave supper, I was sleeping with the T.V. News. Alone, settled, yet afraid that I did not truly understand the term "The mountain." What I forgot to do was check on when the next managers meeting with the managers, and the board was scheduled. Not for a month or so was my wish, but I wrote a note to myself to put that in the number one check list spot.

I could not be denied that meeting. Mr. Masterson was strange yet as he said I knew he and I would meet again. What did he expect? I started looking for the history of his life, and the business, to help with preparation for that meeting. Planning ahead did not make too much sense but tomorrow I had to look at seven wings of a business building without even knowing the name of the chief of each wing.

I fell into a difficult night of rest after a long but hot shower. Missing Love and the short walk also caused me to wonder. What would tomorrow be like? Let me see, 15 to 25 minutes to get to work, a stop for coffee and donut, a flower for Carol's desk, a note for the date of the next quarterly meeting, and a clean shirt and tie.

Rest, or sleep, and time to remain alert for the next step upward, on a very very tall mountain and I was at the base of it. Climbing one step, one day at a time. How high could I go now? What day would tomorrow be? Oh no, it is only Wednesday. This is a 31-day month.

Things to See, To Do and to Be

Arrival at 07:30 was easy, for me, however getting into the building with no key was not. Pushing the door access key button, a guard came to it and ask me for my I.D. Settled in to the room I was surprised to see Carol already there. Coffee, with cream and sugar, was in the office as well as a current daily newspaper. What a start.

Exactly at eight, we left the administration wing and my first question was obviously stupid. I do not even know everyone in that room and I am not the boss, or am I? Why did I get promoted from shipping to administration and get placed in Mr. Masterson's office? Carol said left or right at the first location. I said you choose and I will follow. What a decision.

She went left and of course I went thinking why? We were at door blue "legal." Why? Was it the most important place to start? Entering the room, the first request I had was to photograph the room from the door. The second thing I wanted to know was how many work here?

Leaving the first room and crossing the hallway, we stepped into the black and white door which was labeled "sales." I asked the same things. On to door number three down the main hall walking towards the mountain. We stopped at the left door labeled "short sleeves." Same things I said. Once again moving down the longer hallway we saw the door marked "All blue—contractors." Same pictures please, same information. Across the hallway, the room marked "Short sleeve—networks." This was a mightily long hallway. The next to the last area hall was slightly different and the floor and the doors and walls were all a green color. Arrival at the door placed me in somewhat of disruption. It was marked "Green Coats–Financial." Straight ahead was the door and a different hallway, with a large sign with the number two in the center–also known as "shipping." Why did this area have the different hallway? Turing on the light, I stepped into the hallway and there in front of the door was Mr. Masterson. He said "Welcome to the starting point of "The Mountain."

Asking Carol, she said oh yes, I forgot to tell you, Mr. Masterson, when he was boss always came to work at 7:00 a.m. He likes sugar in his coffee and the newspaper open to the last page where the marriage and death notices were published.

We walked back toward administration and I ask Carol to have the managers or boss staff meet us in the conference room and to bring their notebooks. This was another day, and it was as I saw it.

Asking Mr. Masterson to sit at the desk he said "no", I would rather stand by the window and look up at the mountain. The sun is in a good location now and once again I might see the two birds over the top. "What a day this would be…"came into my head. Where were those song words?

John said, "Jim, may I be straight?" I said "yes sir." He said "I hired you or moved you from shipping location to my office on purpose. It was not because you saved my dog or because we met at the coffee shop. It was because you used the mountain, climbing as I have done so many times in the past, and each time you did, you looked at the decision points of the pathway with concerns that were placed there by God's Word in your life. My bible was left here because God said for me to tell the next person to lead by the book and remember the reason why it was placed where we could see it."

The book in and of itself, was just a book, unless the cover was touched and the next paragraph, with the words, were looked at. Reading, is part, but hearing the word that was read is another part.

There are 130 verses in the KJV bible that speak or have the word "mountain." There is a history to this business written in the pathway "The Mountain." Walk the pathway and read the book. Use it to govern the meeting with the branch chiefs and remember "Love."

What A Day That Will Be

Mr. Masterson said "Welcome to the staff. Today I need three statements from each of you. You know I will give you the statements as you stand, but will not give them to you in order. "They are "Give a summary of your current situation, Development made to arrive at current situation, and state of alternative strategies."

We have eight wings in this building. They are simple and easy to understand or visualize.

Administrative – 12; Shipping – 4; Legal – 7; Sales – 5; Contractors – 9; Networks – 6; Financial – 7 and an empty wing.

A total of 50 employed people when we had 1 person when the building was first generated into existence and over the last 100 years. A 50% reduced force with less than anything that could be easily called "The Mountain."

I have met Mr. Sherman, and he has accepted his assignment from shipping department to the administrative office which changes things a little. The mountain has not had a change. Mr. Sherman today you will take part in the 50 people's lives and the existence for "The mountain." Welcome!

"Thank you, Mr. Masterson." I stood and walked slowly around the room. I noticed that many of them had noting identifiable on their notepad. I asked Carol how many people had passed away in listing of today's paper and how many had been born today. She said "7 passed and 9 were born." Then I said "We now have a need to gain the trust of two more people."

"As part of the organization that is about to reclaim the mountain, each department has a challenge, and each has a stepping place to be noticeable.

"Stand up and face each other. Do you know the truth about the need of the person or persons you are looking at? Why is it not being done by you and your staff as part of your reason for being here? If it fails on a time that you are being paid, then you help us fall from the mountain.

"This point in life came to me because on a given day I stopped my vehicle, had a rest at the local refreshment location, and then walked to the bottom entrance point of the mountain. Each department's staff and purpose are there now. Change the name on your door, change the color of the room, change the location of the desk within the room, but change your heart into a group of people able to climb the mountain each and every day."

After the office was dismissed and the supervisors left, Mr. Masterson said: "I will be in touch." You have access to the power to do that which is necessarily needed to endeavor the climb and see the staff within reach of each step.

Walking with him toward the door he turned and said "I have a pair of climbing spikes if you need them." Smiling,

I wondered about that statement. I saw Love coming to him and jumping up to be touched. What a day that will be when my Jesus I shall see. These words were strong in the view of Mr. Masterson leaving the office building.

Knowing the truth of each moment, and each hour of each day, would be something special if you did not wonder why you had forgotten or did not know. The special time of Love visible to the source of your time with thinking straightened. Why is it that when we are held accountable to the moment of time, when there is a difference in the knowledge of truth, is it important to measure the way we stand secure? In the open time of breath there is a moment when we realize that even the time of a small dog in your life, can tell you the truth about how you might have ignored the time of yesterday. The Time, the Truth, and the Love.

Starting Somewhere

Asking Carol to hold any calls, and to set up the conference room for a meeting with the administrative staff, I entered the office and sat down. The chair appeared to be related to peace and quiet. Not understanding that, I looked out the window at the mountain and it seemed to say "Welcome home."

My mind seemed at perfect peace and yet there was a force that had entered into it. That force was also known as the past.

Beginning somewhere would be a great idea, if you knew for certain where somewhere was. Not that it makes a difference, but it is a beginning part of life.

Now then, having opened the past, into a place of existences, what should, or could be next? Wondering about that, or if, or when, next might appear is a good place to start.

The initial attempt to write was something called "The Word" and what was intended as an easy accomplishment turned into something very difficult, because in the later stages of the concept, it was thought to be ready to be published and then the stop of life came into existence and several hundred dollars later, it was still on the shelf with a lot of maybes.

Then, the idea of something else in a different format came into existence and it was called, or started out with the name of, "The Pond," and ended with the name of, "The Storm." Now here we are together with either of them in the hold status of life and a third document being generated.

Able to write from here, and able to store to a backup portable backup drive gives this perhaps an increase in life. What would it be like to takes parts of the first attempt, and the second attempt and place them into existence here. Problem number one, the paragraphing of this document was "center" and the others are "left side" Cut and paste seems like a good idea and perhaps that is the way other books have been put together.

Tonight I went to a used book store and read the opening paragraphs of five different books. Each was interesting, and each, slightly different, and here I am in between all of them.

The book 'The Word" started with the idea of "In the Beginning" of course found in the KJV bible as Genesis 1:1. So much of my life is attached to that single starting point, that this entire book perhaps could be centered on that single thought.

The second change became known, as previously mentioned, as "The Pond" changing into "The Storm." Because of the change, it was blended into the reasoning of understanding what the "beginning" was part of. Very quickly, I begin to notice the damage that had been done by the Encephalitis of eight years prior. Keeping things in a position of correct relationship now is definitely a beginning. (See Appendix A).

Installing new software to a computer, and getting a new or third book started, and putting all of it together along with backup email capability, was quiet a successful accomplishment.

Then I am learning what I should remember. That aside, I still struggled with the title for the writing, as well as wondering why the first two were not in print and being sold? Thus the title.

Hearing the knock on the door, I snapped back into reality and smiled at Carol. Sorry I said, the past had shown up. She said, the administrative staff is ready to meet and the front door is temporarily, unless you want "LOVE" to guard it, locked.

Getting paid for the action or the requirement to lead by example—the staff was waiting for what they might expect. We were moving into reality. That was at least the concept of thought. Moving into it.

Moving into Realty

When the clock sounded its beep or reminder, I noticed that it was 4:00 p.m. Time to watch the crew start the leaving process. Perhaps to learn more about what or why I was in the front office.

Shipping left first, and I was not surprised. Yet why did one of the legal team leave? What was on her mind. Was it something I should remember. My mind began to drift back again.

Each hour seemed like an eternity and nothing could be more distance from the beginning of the desire to know when the storm would arrive. What type of storm, how and where to be, when the storm arrived?

Another beginning time that is difficult to instill within myself, and yet I know, that there is a storm coming.

Now perhaps a time to wonder about the past and where the difficulty began. Remembering the day standing at the eastern edge of the pond, and watching the waves, ever so slight move from the south to the north, and an occasional bug touching the water, and a fish jumping towards it, will always be a place that I can remember being at the beginning of the fear of a storm. This was a recent past.

Going further back in the past, a place that I stood was not a pond, just a lowering of the level of mother earth and looking away, towards the fence line, a wondering of why this part of the property was so difficult to deal with. Perhaps I was even then wondering if a storm, unwanted, could be in the future. Perhaps even there, a time to think ahead, yet failing to do so because of being content to stand in a place, without wondering about the future. Seems like a piece of classical music that is not understood and yet acceptable to hear. Wanting to see more and know more about the beginning place for the fear of this coming storm.

Leaving the area of the local existing pond, I can wonder about the distance to the next destination. Within me is a desire to stay located in one place, yet also a strong desire to move away from where I am standing, because the storm is coming and it will be impacting not only my life, but many other people that I do not even know. What time is it? Early morning? Or near lunch?

Does it matter when the distance to the next step is a step in the process of getting ready for the walk that will always be remembered? The next step will be one that could be thought of in the future and seen in the past, yet it will be remembered because someone mentioned the storm.

When I want to think about why, or when, or where, there is always the wondering of not remembering the reason. What day was the first? What time was the worst?

Do I even remember that there was a time and place that the fear of the coming storm began?

Only when I stop long enough to look at a cloud, watch it move and change, do I wonder how big the possibility of the time will be when there is no long ever a possibility of a storm. Then the touch of air moving across my body reminds me that I am standing in the presence of time and there must be a reason.

Then the day started as I woke because my youngest dog wanted to be noticed. Outside was a needed place, and the time was now. Constant in reminding me that the door must be opened, the light turned on, the rug worn, and the walk through the house to the outer door, each time helps me to remember that there is time, and that time existed before the storm. When then do I thank the dog?

Do I even stop to think about that, or do I just want her to finish her need so that I can go back to bed and escape? Each conflict in time, of the past, from when I first remember the storm.

The intercom startled me into reality and I was once again waking to something from the past. Why? I said "yes, Carol, what? She reminded me that the office staff was pleased that I did not find fault with them and she had a list of changes they had suggested to the process of the "Mountain."

One of them struck her interest. Draw or define a picture of the "top" of the mountain and give it a name.

Thinking about that would be a great challenge for Thursday, and wanting to know who, I put it aside until

I could come up with a picture of what that "top" looked like to a business that was in the process of falling or degrading again. We did have 12 in the front office and it could be reduced to six. What does that picture look like? When should it appear on the big mountain board in front of our building. Why or what would it do?

Perfection

Given any day of a working week, would a leader want to make an impression of the upcoming, last day of a week? Would truth, or fiction, or arrangement be the issue of what the employee knew or would think, walking to the door on a Friday, knowing that there was a mountain visible within sight?

Thinking back to my past life with the Air Force and my 23.5 years of service, I wondered if that was part of my thinking. The fact is, that was not the end of life.

I had a two-year separation in to something called retirement when I figured out that 38 was too young to stop thinking about life. Moving then into reality, the search for perfection came into existence, in a stronger way.

Walking across what could be called retirement into a new look at life was not announced, yet it was reality. I was troubled. Thinking about now was not strongly present, yet neither was thinking about the future.

Doing it all over again and knowing for sure that it helps to remember why. The distance between each step and the time between start and stop is only a thought at the moment, yet the need for remembrance is strong. Why did I struggle with the distance of the past?

Sometime, there will be a period of setting in the easy chair and doing nothing except waiting. In that period of time the thought of a possible storm comes and goes and the need to remove it by drifting into another place such as hoping the telephone will ring, or that the truck that just passed the window was an unauthorized truck for our residential street, even that escape for the moment does not totally allow the distant storm to leave.

Pause, think it through, wonder why, but know for sure that the distance between this time and the next is possibly shorter, but hopefully longer. Cold weather tonight, sleeping a little longer in the morning, all of which will be better than wondering.

Can it be that there is an answer to the total question of time? Will the necessity of knowing the answer to that excuse the need for explanation of why the cloud is so strong in my vision at the present time?

The reason for wonder is a good place to stop and think about the possibility of distance between my wanting no storm and the fact that dealing with a storm in the future will be part of life.

Sometime there will be an answer to the question, but, without a time to measure that thought, only a cloud passing over which cannot be seen during the dark of night, and the wind blowing causing me to remember that there are clouds moving, will be sufficient to think about tomorrow and the existence of another period of time. Do not think for a moment that the concept of a storm has left me.

The reason that Carol reminded me that all of the staff and crew had left except for security bugged me back into the night before a Friday. What would be necessary for me to show the people, the staff, and the mountain that Friday was important?

I asked Carol to come in for a short memo to the wings for release at 9:00 the next day. She settled into the office chair with a smile, and said, "Has Love been talking to you?" Embraced, or wondering, I did not have an answer to that question.

Memo: Staff: What does Friday mean? Is it something you should remember, or is it something that is not noticeable for the past few days? Report your concept in the next quarterly meeting, or put a memo on the hallway boards. "Manager!"

"Carol, can I take you to an early supper at the without asking stage?" She smiled and said "No, but thank you for asking." I wondered why she said no.

The walk out to the car and a thought of going to a lift apartment, was troubling, especially without the dog, "Love," to greet me.

Perhaps, climbing a part of the mountain would not be a bad idea. At least I knew the first part was steep and in the coming of darkness could be or would be more difficult. Then I was in between.

The mountain was very present in the day to day visibility of the building and the reason for its existence. The sun sitting behind it proved something.

Beginning Storm

Remembering Friday, the last day of my first full boss office work was now here. Why did I think about this day being so significant? Friday is a six letter word and we only worked a five-day week. What was the difference? Just one day. Wondering what this was about made me want to resist going back in the thinking process. Suddenly my past interrupted.

Thinking back, Dad Peas, held my hands as I watched my mother leave. I am not sure if she was driving the car or if she was a passenger that day. Dad Peas, the foster father dad, spoke to me in a strong voice and said "Let's go gather eggs." Not even sure of what that was, I trudged along and went into the place where chickens were. He removed a basket from the nail, and placed it in my left hand. Showing me how, he reached under a chicken and took the egg out and placed it into the basket.

Then he said: "you do it." Still wondering why, I was afraid not to, yet wanted to prove even though I did not know at my age of three, I could be a man just like him. Reaching under the next chicken there was no egg that I could feel, so dad Peas moved me to the next chicken laying. Reaching under I felt the egg and removed it from where it was laying.

The chicken pecked me on the hand and I dropped the egg and it broke. Dad Peas said, "Tomorrow you will not eat breakfast." I remember crying as dad Peas took me to the house I had not even been in.

Now fear, as well as hunger, troubled me. Then I saw others in the room. A large but clean person, who as a woman made me see that I did not recognize her, yet some reason I felt that she would be called mother. It was a short thinking process, as she turned and said to me "I am Mom Peas, wash your hands and pick up your muddy feet."

You need to learn how to come into the kitchen if you want to be part of this family. Once again, I began to cry, but this time I was placed in a corner of the larger room and told to stand there.

The time that passed seem like forever, yet when a boy who was older and stronger told me to follow him I was afraid not to. He took me up the stars into what I learned was referred to as the "loft" and showed me my place to sleep.

He also showed me a place to put my dirty cloths, and told me that he would show me where the bedroom or "outhouse" was. He then led me down the stairs and for some reason I wanted to count them, but he would not go that slow.

Outside the kitchen door and what seemed like a long way was another place. He said "you can always hide in here." Oh what I remember about the first day.

The next morning, hearing a call from down stairs mom Peas said, "Rise and shine" It is time to do your chores. I redressed as best I could and hurried down, almost falling in the stairwell toward the bottom door and wondered why they did not let me sleep until I wanted to get up.

Then the boy took me by the hand back to the chicken coop and I remembered the chicken that hurt me and I wanted to make sure I did not drop any of the eggs. This time I made sure and going to the house I ask quietly if I would get to eat.

Things were passed in front of me, yet that boy put stuff on my plate and told me to sit up. White stuff he called "grits" and eggs he called "good" and a biscuit and glass of something he called cow juice. Then I was told to bless the meal and did not know what that was either. The boy leaned toward me and said "just thank your God for our food"! He reached under the table and pinched me. I quickly said "Thank you God for food." Grabbing my fork and rushing towards the eggs, I was hungry.

What could be better than eggs? Not the grits, for sure, but I did like the cow juice and wondered about why they called it that. Leaving the table, and wondering, I was taken outside once again and this time I noticed the sun coming up and the other buildings around us. Wanting to run away was certainly a plan that I begin to hang on to. Not knowing for sure which direction I could run was the reason I decided at the moment that walking towards the tractor was a good idea.

How big it was. Why did I want to ride it? When would I be able to drive it? All of the sudden, the loss of time, or the beginning of a new day was there.

Inside the barn door was a smell that was truly different. The cows, standing close by and the rooster moving away from me, and the smell of something that did not seem to be good, was there. Inside the barn, as a boy, I wondered why the time seemed so important.

Asking for permission, I wanted to ride the tractor and being told that I had to earn the right was a strange but thinkable wonder. I can do it. I can do it, came into my wanting and made the fear of a storm disappear for a while.

Where does that ladder go? I asked. To the loft and future for your age to grow into was the reply. What did that mean, and why could I not just climb the stairs? Odd the light now shining though the upper window made the smell of cows and stuff even smell better, and the fear of not knowing or wanting to find a way of escape was drifting towards the storm of my life and seemed to quiet the distance for now.

What do you mean, that I will have to shovel the cow stuff out into the barn yard? I can try, but I am not sure why. I do not know what a fork is. The fork had four prongs on it, and they had stuff stuck to them.

What did he mean, for me to clean the stall? Why did the cow moo? Why in the world was picking eggs looking like more fun? Then dad Peas came into the barn and told the boy to take me to the garden. There I was introduced to a "row" that was mine to work, and the rule was easy to remember. "Weeds in the row, means you do not eat." What is a weed? Why do I feel the storm coming again?

Once again the intercom buzzer startled me back into reality. It was a long distance call from someone in New York wanting to talk to the company leader. Why me? Carol, put them on hold for a minute while I got a dictionary, or a personnel roster.

The Sun Rise

Friday night TV was worthless because of the continuation of troubled thinking. Not sure why but my youth and my past seemed to be in control of my now. The past life of my childhood was still strongly in me and my wondering, thinking, problems,

Time forward to a place, where even the process of gathering eggs has been changed, given to another person and my assignment now was to livestock, or work the process of making animals do what they are there for. One day, near the evening time, dad Peas noticed that one of the cows was absent from the return home time. He instructed three of us to go into the pasture and locate the cow and head it towards home. Running, laughing, and hoping for the best the three of us went to the west side of the farm towards the watering hole.

There she was, stuck in the middle of the pond, with her bag full and her legs unmovable. She was stuck. One went to inform dad Peas that the cow was stuck and the other two of us decided that we could get her out. Removing our shoes and pants we waded into the pond, sinking down into the mire.

No wonder she was stuck. We were up to our knees already and could not coach her to step out. Then, we thought if we scare her, we will get her to move upon the dryer part so we yelled and hollered, yet nothing seemed to work. Dad Peas showed up with the tractor and a long rope. Told us what to do and how, slowly but surely the cow was freed from trouble.

Having to escort her back to the barn, I was haunted by the fact that one of us would be late for supper because she had to be milked beforehand. Taking a bet on why, we argued all the way back with me winning the "do not milk" part but still be stuck with the process of herding her back and cleaning up the lazy cow from the pond mud.

Fall had arrived and we began to enter into harvest time. Getting crops into the barn, the loaf, the hay and corn picked, and the pigs rounded up was all part of what was to be the next major turning point in my life.

Not having been to the slaughter, or not being warned that it was also a huge part of time, was a brand new experience. Perhaps riding the tractor was not so important after all. I did not want to be the person who had to kill a pig, or even, the next chicken that we might eat. I did have my principles to defend.

The work force from neighboring farms gathered for the day and we began at day break to harvest the work of the farm. Setting out the maple tree equipment to gather the drip of the line into buckets, we moved them into the process of getting surpass.

Picking the blue berries and the apples seemed much more enjoyable. Still, very deep inside, was the desire to be able to drive the tractor and be able to move the plow, or the wagon, or even just have fun getting it into the barn for the end of a busy day.

As the harvest went on, and the work was accomplished, we then had more time to wonder about life, play with each other, and think about another time. The time which I can remember is the fall trip from the farm to the church. I did not know what a church was, or where it was at, or why we were going there so early in the morning. Hooking up the wagon with two horses and getting the baskets of harvest loaded into the wagon seem like so much work.

Dad Peas was strong and quiet, yet he seemed to be excited in a different way. The help that was part of the harvest, and even I, loaded into the wagon and left for a trip that I had never made before, and would always remember. As we got closer to the church one of the boys said "last year I rang the bell." He seemed to be the only one that was able to run alongside of the wagon and sing.

Why did he seem to be so happy? The distance to the church narrowed and I became very much aware of the tower over the church and the desire to be the first to ring the bell. No wonder fall was a special time. Ringing the church bell seemed to be the only reason such hard work was wanted. Yes, I actually was able to ring the bell and was rewarded by the preacher with smile and a hug. I think to this day, I will remember how wonderful the trip to the church, the fellowship, the food, and the sound of the bell was. The trip back to the farm was something to remember.

THE MOUNTAIN

Winter was perhaps something to have in your thought process, but snow? Why even wonder about that? One day, awakened at the sound of the bell, dad Peas said to climb "out" and go gather the eggs and milk the cows.

What in the world was the "climb out" for? Then it was apparent, the only way to the chicken coop or the barn was out the second story window into about 3 and a half feet of snow drifts. Now tractor driving was definitely out of the picture.

So was getting eggs or milking cows. Why not just build a big snowman and play? Not too far there was a hill that would be fun to slide down using the piece of wood that we called our sled. Oh yes, winter had arrived and in some way the storm was remembered again.

Change Coming

Dad Peas, ask me to go to the barn with him. He said there was something that I needed to know and he had to tell me. I still am not sure why, or when, he received word that my mother had remarried and was about to come and get me. The time seemed so far away to remember, and yet the storm suddenly began to become visible again. Why? Why now? Who was my new father? When would she get there to pick me up. All of this had rekindled my storm spirit within me and I once again became afraid of the next thing that was to happen. Dad Peas touched me in a way that I had never remembered and he asked me not to tell anyone about it. Time really caused me to wonder. I ran from the barn and looked for a way to escape the news of my mother coming, my mother being married, and most of all my loss of being able to drive the tractor by myself as long as I had permission to take on the next needed responsibility.

My mother and Bob, her husband, arrived the next day. There was little conversation between them and Mr. and Mrs. Peas. For some reason I did not want the next part of my life to become real. That perhaps is another way of saying that I was truly in the storm and afraid that I would not be able to want to wake up again anywhere, or anytime. The drive away from the farm was long and very quiet.

Nothing was said, or nothing I can remember between my new parents and my new home. When we finally arrived I was told my brothers would be there later, and that my other brother and sister were upstairs. Who are they I ask? Nothing was said to explain that Bob had two of his children there or nothing was explained as to why the house was so small, compared to the farm and the barn and the tractor in my life.

All of that was missing and I heard the strange sound of traffic on the street in front of the house. The dog that was there was barking at the cars as thy swept down the street at speed that was unknown to me. The farm was so far away.

Mom showed me the upper bedroom where the children would sleep and she began to prepare our evening meal. Immediately she told me my job was to help in the kitchen and I would be responsible for dish washing and that would help on the cost of all. What else could go wrong? Who were my brothers? Where were they? How come they were not there also? Questions to be forever part of my struggle with what the storm would bring.

The day ended with a meal I did not want, and dishes to be done, which I could not know how to do, and most of all a strange place to sleep. After dishes I was sent upstairs to my bed and the floor draft was lit, so I laid down looking for my brothers, and only seeing Bob drinking a beer and watching something called TV.

The next morning, I quickly rose at or just after dawn, thinking about the chores that I no longer had to do and wondering about the reason I did not want to know more. Time did not matter nor did I even care, but, part of me wanted to get outside and see if I could run away.

I do not remember breakfast that day, but my brother Harvey and my brother David were supposed to be there sometime. Outside, in the immediate area of our house, I disliked what I saw. Bob told me to start cleaning up the trash laying around the yard and put it in the trash can.

One thing at a time, I honestly did not want to do anything here. I slowly allowed myself to wonder and pray so to speak for a way to escape the threat of the storm.

Harvey and David both arrived at the same time in a car that had printing on the side. "Boy's Home" I wondered what that was, or where it was and why they did not go to the farm where I was? Then the dark clouds of a real storm began to show. As they were told to get out, the older boy, Harvey began with some words I have never heard, and Bob immediately grabbed him and told him to "shut up" with that kind of talk.

David kicked Bob and yelled at him, "Let my brother go." So much for being happy. I was totally afraid of everything around me and could not even begin to imagine how five children could live upstairs in the small, no real bed, space, and then it dawned on me that I would have so many more dishes to wash and dry. Why did I have brothers anyway, and who made me wonder about all of this? At nine years old I wanted more than ever to escape the storm.

THE MOUNTAIN

The next day my mother told me to stay inside the house and not to leave. She had to go to work and Bob had already gone. Summer was supposed to be fun but Harvey and David took it as the right time to run away from home. They did not tell me what they were doing and it was several minutes later before they had disappeared.

My half brother and sister were still there, but, even they did not know, or would not say where Harvey and David went.

That night a policeman was at the house talking with my mother and Bob and I was sent upstairs. The night was very difficult and I do not know why but I fell asleep and went into what some call a dream world. The dream was the farm, the cows, the pigs, and the chickens all running away and the tractor would not start.

Then I woke up and made up my mind. I was going to run away from home too. The time was to wait until I could do it without being caught. Would the dog, who was now my friend, follow me? Would the same cop or policeman chase me too? What would it be like to have no place to eat or sleep? Who would care? Perhaps I could find a place with a pond and a place that I could hide away in a storm.

Wanting Sunday to arrive I went to bed and slept again. This time determined to get up, have a light breakfast, and climb on the mountain. I did not want this much change from the past controlling my life in the current way I was. I had started this job as part time and I was not stepping into a leadership position without even knowing the truth. Why? My life past, and my life present were in total collision yet not to be concerned it was that I should remember so that I could learn from the past. My thinking was that even though my life of childhood was coming back it was necessary to learn.

Learning About Time

For some reason the rain woke me at 7:30 a.m. Turing on the TV I looked for a weather channel to see what to expect. After all there was a Monday scheduled so to speak. The weather on channel 3, no, on channel 7, no, where was it. Try channel 14.

A preacher said, why are you in the rain? How did he know? Where did he get off asking me that question? Then he went on to explain there are several different ways of talking about the weather. There are different ways of talking about the bible. For example: When did weather start becoming a problem for someone? Why did it matter? Who would know the truth? Then he mentioned that Scripture again. John 8:32.

That was the most difficult thing, because it kept coming into my life. That one single Scripture. Now I knew that I had something to do in the rain. Looked it up for myself. "You shall know the truth." I thought I always did know that. What is it anyway, besides the fact that it is Sunday, besides the fact that it is raining, besides the fact that I have a job and I sit in a front office, looking like the boss.

What does the truth have to do with all of that? First of all, I had nothing to do with getting into the front office. Something else did. I had no control over the weather and at the point of issue, did not care too much about that. I did have a job. I was getting paid. But, I could not answer the questions that came immediately into my thinking.

Where was the man with the plan? The man who had control of the company, the man who stood on the mountain? The leader, or the man in charge.

Suddenly it stopped raining, the sun came out and the rain stopped. I wanted a cup of coffee and I wanted to climb the mountain to find an answer. Entering the path to the coffee shop the first thing I noticed was the light was beautiful. The smell was wonderful and the day was different. I did want to know more about what the pastor on the TV had said. John 8:32. I wanted to know the truth.

Immediately after coffee and a snack I headed for the mountain time, space and visitation for the climb up to God and the truth about why, when, where, and who. This should be fun. It was only 11:30 Sunday morning and I had the rest of the day.

Without too much concern about the path, I climbed upward until I reached that first turning point on the path. There it was, Left or Right? Why? What would matter if I turned left or I turned right? I would still be walking somewhere. As if to answer my question, or my thinking suddenly out of nowhere Mr Masterson appeared. "Hi Jim, getting older?"

"Mr. Masterson, how did you get up here"? His reply was, "I was climbing in the rain. Saw it starting to clear and started down for time sake to be here now. He knew you and I would be here"

Who is the "he you are talking about?" was my next question. He said: "What are you breathing and where does it come from?" I stood amazed at the fact that I was breathing, but true I did not fully understand how to reply.

Remember, when I told you that the bible I left in the office was for you to read? I was totally honest with him. "I do remember, but I have not read it very much." He said: Monday, read Genesis 1:1 and then read the last verse. Two thing you need to know. A place to start and a place to stop.

He said, "continue to climb for a while, you will wonder about this for a while. You need to know that HE is watching you climb and He knows if you are going up or down."

Looking at the sun, feeling the wind, suddenly Mr. Masterson had disappeared. He was gone and I was on the mountain. He was gone and I was hungry, thirsty, and alone. Or was I?

Monday Again

Starting out for work, I thought of driving because there was a very light snow, early for our November. Something said to walk, so I started down the stairs and out. Walking the short way towards the coffee shop I noticed immediately that Love was outside, lying. I started to cross the street then looked at my watch. This time I was going early enough to get to work before Carol.

Walking quickly and thinking about Monday again, I wondered. If 2 plus 2 equals four, then why does Monday seem so different at times? Over and over again, I wondered why Mr. Masterson was at the coffee shop. What did that mean to me or to The Mountain?

Arriving early, I noticed Carol's car was not in the parking lot, so I thought I had been able to be first, other than security. Using my entrance card I entered the building and stepped into the hallway. Fred, the security guard said "hello, Mr. Sherman."

Stepping around the hallway I entered the office. There was Carol. At her desk, and busy. Entering my office, there was the newspaper, the coffee and a small tray of business mail on the right hand corner. Sitting quickly, I noticed a yellow sticker within the pages of the newspaper. Instead of going to the section I liked best, I saw on the page that was marked: "The Mountain needs climbing" as a headline article. Pouring my coffee, I noticed my hand shake.

Once again my mind began to drift. Why was that so prevalent in the office. I looked in the pile of things in the basket: An office memo saying Mr. Johnson, Legal wanted a meeting today, a request form from shipping to interview and or hire two workers, and the financial quarterly statement for "The Mountain." Looking at the bottom line, it was not a pleasant sight for a company working and having 50 employees. It was Monday.

Once again my memory started to shift. Life continued with little or no communication as to what was really happening. Bob would sit at night watching TV. Mom was there. Both were silent and not seemingly aware that I was there or not there. More than ever I wanted to run away from home. I was scheduled to grow up so to speak and move into high school. Perhaps something would be better there and I wondered if. Then the call was received that Harvey and David had been located in Kansas at a farm working.

They were arrested and returned to Michigan, where dad Peas would have seen to it they were punished hardily, Bob just seemed to let it pass that they were home. Little did he know that they had already planned to leave again.

They ask me to play a game at the house with a B.B. Gun. I was to pretend I had been shot and they would take care of calling the police. If this was a game they did not give it a name. I did not want to play and without knowing why, or how, I pointed the gun at Harvey and pulled the trigger. It went off and the BB hit him between the eyes and I locked the front door and ran to the back locking it.

He said he would pay me back and left with David. Little did I know that was their plan. Thinking that I would be caught and punished, I decided to run away myself. Leaving the house, cutting through the lots around the block I found my way to the river bridge and thought that would be a good place to hide. My mother found me and took me back home. How did she know where I would hide? Turns out that was not the first time a child did something that silly.

Dad and Mom were volunteer fire department staff and anytime there was a local fire they would leave and stay gone. I used that time to get further and further from the house. Walking one day I thought I would cut through between a store to the next block.

There in plain site was a pack of coca-coca bottles. Wow, what a find. I grabbed them and took them to the store across the street to cash in my collection of bottles. Got caught doing that because that was where the owner put their returns.

This time I was taken to jail by the local police and placed in a holding cell. Friday, Saturday, and Sunday I was alone with no contact until late Sunday evening. Bob picked me up and told me to get into the car. He drove me home with one thing on his mind. Show me who is boss.

He ripped me with a belt in the backside multiple times and warned me that this would be the last time. He said I would know what he meant. Age 16 was a hard age to be away from the farm, and looking away at the storm that was very visible.

I noticed that the step-father was a loner as long as no one messed with his beer drinking time and mom seemed to be locked in the Detroit Baseball games.

Then I wondered what I could do to be gone more and homeless. I went to the bowling alley, where mom bowled on Tuesday and Thursday nights and found out I could work there.

Starting out upstairs on the single isle side of life, I learned how to sit bowling pins, eat my profits, and break even four nights a week.

Mom did not seem to care and then I learned that the real money was sitting two alleys side by side, in league nights down stairs. I asked for permission to try it out one day, and did good enough they hired me that night, Friday. What a deal, now I was up town and in sight of a real future.

One night I saw two blue suited airman bowling, and while I was waiting for the league to start, I watched them and was amazed at the uniforms they wore. Asking them how they told me if I was 17 I could enlist in the Air Force. Only 16, I wondered because my birthday was still weeks away.

That night I got to sit mom's team's game and I helped her get a great score, each time she threw the ball. She was so amazed had how good she did. Taking me home that night, I asked her. Can I joint the Air Force? She said she would check into it.

The next day she had me go with her and we saw a man who said he was to be "My Sergeant" and I should learn to say "Yes, Sir"! I did that loud and clear. Mom signed some papers and I was told that I was official a member of the U.S.A.F. To be at the train station the next mooring at 4:00 a.m. To board the train to boot camp. What is boot camp? How come I won't be 17 until next Tuesday? Where is California?

Now I know that the farm was further than ever away from me and what seemed like a storm was getting closer to me. On the train the next day, there was a guy who said he was in charge of us and he told us to sit down, shut up and pay attention. Within 10 minutes of the train starting up, he was playing black jack with 5 other boys and seemed to be winning. So much for my leader. So much for mom and Bob. I was in the Air Force and would be 17 in one more day.

The train trip to California, in some ways, was something that helped settle my concern for the storm that was in my life. The space and beauty of the land held my attention as the train went click, click. Three days of being somewhat locked up bothered me, and yet there was the desire to know more, to get somewhere new, and to be secure.

The feeling was hiding me from the threat of the storm. Little did I even realize that the clouds were always visible, and the passing of the distance in the time of life was going to be remembered. When the train entered the mountain range and began to slow down, slower and slower it was a time when even then, I wanted to jump off and be free.

THE MOUNTAIN

The buzzer on the desk intercom rang and woke me out of a distant place. My past was strongly staying present, and it seemed to always want to start on Mondays. Carol said it was the caller from New York again, presently asking to speak. I took my tablet and pen and switched the line. "Hello, this is Mr. Sherman, how can I help you"?

Incoming Considerations

"Hello, may I ask who's calling?" "This is Mr. Jason, from ABC." "We have been trying to touch base with you because of our visit to your area on Wednesday of this week?

"Can we have an appointment for Wednesday? I will have one of our people with me and if you want you can also ask Mr. Masterson."

It was like a snow storm had suddenly blown onto the mountain. I thanked Mr. Jason and hung up the telephone. On the intercom, I asked Carol to come in. She entered the room and I ask her to shut the door. Telling her I noticed her car was missing this morning I ask if I could help. She said it was being worked on and would be brought to her before 4:00. Thank you. What a day today has been, and it is only Monday. "Ask Mr. Allen to come up. Thanks."

Mr. Allen knocked on the office door and entered as if he owned the office. I did not invite him to sit. "What is your problem, Mr. Allen?" He said "She wants to quit, and all I ask her was not to quit the union." "What is the problem, I said?" "Her boyfriend works for a different location and they are mad at the union there also. It is just internal, to the requirements the union makes, on them I think."

"Let her fill out the papers and give her a 90-day completion time to consider it." "If she is still anxious then let it go." "That's all."

All of this happened on Monday, before lunch? Why? As Mr. Allen left the office my mind began to drift again to the past.

The Air Force base we were sent to was no longer part of the Air Force command however, I remember that first day and the impact that it had on my life so very well. The MTI assigned to us let us know, right away that we were his, and we would learn about "Yes, SIR." The first day, after three days of travel seemed to last forever.

Tired both of the time of travel and the lack of understanding, the Storm of change in season of life, was very strong. Wanting to be something, but not even knowing how to march. Not knowing how to count out loud, hut, two, three, four or was it Hut, Two, Three, Four? It was so hard to move from the bus that we road into the base on, to the barracks, that we would call "Yes Sir." The fun of it, or remembering it in the now of my life is something that reminds me that even big storms can mellow down to an enjoyable remembrance.

Boot camp was 16 weeks of things that we had no idea would happen to us. For example, the first week was something called KP and we got to wash pots and pans. It seemed like the dishes would never stop getting dirty. I remember saying the wrong thing to the wrong person and got put in the potato punishment place. Peeling, peeling, peeling and wondering just how many potatoes they wanted for breakfast? Who knew they would also want them for dinner or that thing they called chow.

After the week of KP we were moved off into something called boot camp training where we learned to make a bed, pack our cloths into squares of a few inches and place them into the "foot locker" where the Sergeant could dump them out and tell us to do it again, and again, and again. Why could they not just leave the cloths in the "foot locker?" By the way, I found out my foot locker knew the way to the ground, from the second story of the thing call our barracks. Also found out how many times I could run to the ground and bring my foot locker up and then one thing of my cloths to the foot locker. Lots of practice doing that.

The 16 weeks seemed to rush by and we marched in a parade and saw the flag in front of us until we rounded the one-mile parade. Immediately after we got back to the barracks we were yelled at to "get out" and "get ready" for "field training." Where in the world could there be a field outside of our door? We soon found it about 3 miles away and we got to run most of that way to the place where we would sleep on the ground, all day, sing songs in the firing range, and listen to the instructor teach us how to "love" our rifle. Then we finally got to shoot it. I think I remember being afraid of the "storm" once gain.

After field training, we actually "shipped out" and were hurried to something they called "our" school. For me and some others it was a place called "Kessler AFB" and that was another chance to learn what it meant to do KP. The first week the pots and the pans and the potatoes were still very much in my life. Morse Code School and

Radio School was 13 weeks of learning to say "yes Sir" in a new way.

Morse code was rated in what was referred to a "groups per minutes" and the first thing we did was learn each letter of the alphabet. After learning the rhythm of the letter A ."_" and the letter "B" _... etc. we were told to master each speed group. Two words per minute, four words per minute and so on.

Getting to sixteen was really easy but a "wall" of resistance hit me there, and I was stuck with failing that group twice. I was told that if I failed it again, I could not apply for "ground air radio" training and that I would be forced out of "communications" into cook school. Then I remember something someone said when I was a child at the summer bible school class. Pray!

Not knowing what it really meant to pray I said, "GOD help me." He did and I passed the 16 GPM class the next day and moved upward in training.

The first weekend pass after graduation was called a "town pass" and we were told to put on our "class A" uniform and get the pass to go on the bus into town. We were excited to see something other than the four walls of our barracks, and the four wall of the Morse code class room. A group decided to go to town and get drunk. That was the plan. We boarded the bus and went into town and we were told to be back at the bus stop at 17:00 hours. Huh? How can you have liberty in just a little over 4 hours of "freedom?" The very first stop was to find a bathroom but when we got there, there was a sign on the door saying "No black." What did that mean? There were no black guys in our flight. There were no black guys in the school, there were no black guys. Why was that sign on the wall? Little did we know even then that another kind of "storm" was building.

Looking for a way to get a beer, and finding out we were not old enough, and knowing there was nothing to call fun, we wandered the streets of Mississippi looking for what it met to be "on leave." Why did the Air Force not have that in boot camp?

Back at the base, we were told that some things had happened and we would be sent to our "first" duty assignment. The top student would be allowed to pick theirs, the rest of the class would be sent somewhere. I was told that I was going to "Kwajalein Island." What was that? Another boot camp? Or was it just a new way of saying "Storm?"

Carol touched the intercom button and reminded me it was 4:30. I was still lost in the past with a meeting I did not want on Wednesday and needing Mr. Masterson to be part of the moment.

Decision Thinking Time

Walking home toward the loft, I was able to wonder about some things that troubled my thinking. My past kept coming to me strongly. My past was just that, past. Nothing serious but still, past.

Then I notice that Love was laying by the center window, and urgency came into my mind as I went over the street in the snow. Stopping long enough to pet her, I went in and saw Mr. Masterson at the table he was usually at. I ask if I could join him. He motioned to the waiter, and she brought both of us coffee.

Mr. Masterson said, "I had a visitor this morning" He wanted to buy me out at a reasonable price and offered some extras for me to consider. Wanting to have all 55 percent of "The Mountain."

I asked if the man was from NY. Mr. Masterson said, how did you know? I told him of the meeting call that I had for Wednesday, an ask if he could be in it. He said "more me to listen to them" and asked for decision making time. Other than that we chatted and had coffee and watched the snow come down.

I walked back to a timely welcome but continued in the past of my life. Getting to go was exciting, however, wanting to go was part of the storm. My return to the pass was even stronger now.

Not knowing anything about where it was, I was excited to "fly" in an Air Force plane and I actually got to sit up with the pilot and co-pilot where the radio was. Listening to the guy that was assigned to that spot, I thought I had finally gotten rid of the "storms" in my life and that if I was excited you probably saw it in me.

After many hours of what seemed long, I was told we were about to land on Kwajalein. I looked out the window and ask the radio operator, "where is it?" He said "right down there." I looked again and could not see an airport. Old well, the storm was back again. And the pilot told me to go strap myself in for the "landing would be" ruff.

Not exactly sure about the year, but I think it was in the 1957 time period that life or as I call it here, the storm, began to change. There was not much to do "on the job" so to speak. We had just two large rooms in the building, and the work area was set into three different section. Radio airway, mores code, and teletype. The center of the room was open and that is where our world (or the boss) over saw all of us poor guys that had to do the job. Starting out as the newest airman, I got the good stuff, like empty the trash, and make the coffee and clean the equipment.

Morse code had four different frequencies that we monitored and the easy one was the point to point, from Kwajalein to Guam. Once each hour during the night shift which I started on, we had to do communications check, to the other people on Guam. We would send a simple AK or ",---;-.-" and they would always just send "OK" or "---==.=" back to us. Big job for a radio operator, who wanted to fly, but could not empty trash correct, according to the Sergeant.

As the time went by we were elevated up the latter, so to speak, and I finally got the opportunity to sit at the beginning radio spot. That frequency was the one the aircraft used to communicate with our station on a check, before takeoff, call. Kwajalein, Kwajalein this is AC121 Victory, do you read? What an exciting time to grab the mike and say, "roger, I hear you "5 X 5" even though it was less than ½ mile from the building to where the aircraft was sitting. Moving up in the world of life, and not concerned about a storm.

The time was going by quickly and the exciting part of life was to hear that a talent show was coming to Kwajalein the next night. Stars and music, and WOW stuff, that we had never heard before. What a time. Now that I was 18 I could get a "beer' and party with the guys as we waited to look at the "girls" and yell and scream "take it off" "take it off." Such as it was, three hours later, they were done, boarded the plane and took off to Guam. Leaving Kwajalein was good news. Or was it another "storm?"

Arriving at a placed called "Moses Lake, Washington", 21 radio operators were reporting to the "first sergeant." He said, sign here, and we did and then he told us to go to the building that was to be our dorm and the dining hall was across the triangle. So much for news. The building was empty, no beds, no footlockers and no help.

We flipped a coin to see who would have to go tell the First Sergeant that he was wrong. Later that day, a truck parked in front of the dorm and we begin to unload our stuff. Wondering where, or why, or if we had a job, or would it automatically be another two or three weeks of K.P. The storm.

One week later an officer called us to the original sign in location. We were taken to a location, about 7 miles from the base, in a field where there was one small trailer, and it was all government painted green. We saw the antenna, and the door, and were told that would be our assignment. Once a week a "weather" balloon would be released and we were to monitor its signal until we lost contact! That was it? What a job?

We did not even have a radio check, to do once an hour! What a job. We were told that we would be notified when or if a weather balloon was going to be released, and that on that day, someone had to be at site to monitor that "mission," log in, mark the board with the balloon identification, and wait on the assigned frequency until we heard the balloon send three groups of code for one minute. Then type what we heard, sign off and wait to see if we heard the balloon the next hour.

Seven days a week, 24 hours a day, someone had to sit at that station if a balloon was launched. Our sergeant said that 20 of us had the job, and that he would hold us responsible if he got a bad report. The rest of us argued about who would be the first "on call."

Giving our names, and our opportunity, most of us had a chance to "goof off." Now that was a Storm of a different kind.

Meeting a guy, Dale Watkins, at a skating rink, I got to know him and owners of the skating rink. Found out that if I wanted a job, I could eat free, skate free 7 nights a week and sleep in the loft over the rink. All I had to do was simply work there, and do what I was asked. No sweat G.I. Is the way we said that.

I paid one of the guys to take my shift at the base and started my life away from any type of "storm." Tuesday and Thursday were class dance night.

Dale and I were partners with one of the girls that signed up for the class. Little did I know that the girl Dale started with the first night would someday be my wife. Little did I know that I was so nice, that I would date her sister the first time. What a deal. Tuesday and Thursday, we had regulars and a date. Dale had the car and I had a knack of knowing stuff about "charm" and "smile" and "talk."

One night, Dale's girl was skating too fast on the floor and I had monitor duty that night. I skated up to her, turned around and skated backwards in front of her and asked her why she was skating so fast. The first thing she said to me was "Do you know Jesus?" Goodbye, and I moved away from that frightened by the fact that she could talk, but I could not answer the question.

I did not even know what she said. But something stirred within me. Getting Dale to switch students was easy because Carol's sister, Patty, liked Dale anyway. Now, I had stepped into the very front of what I called the biggest "storm" in life.

As time changed we begin to date on a regular basis after each class and Carol and I would sit in the back seat of Dale's car and the one thing I noticed about Carol was that she was different. We sat together and talked. She had what I needed but I did not know how to even ask about it.

Slowly but surely we began to like each other. Boldly, I asked if I could walk her home from school. Could I see more of her? Would she? There as something about her that made me wonder why she was so different.

The junior prom was coming up and I asked her if she would dance with me if I went and I wanted to take her to it. What a step. I entered into her life in an almost formal way, to get closer to her and even perhaps to get her to "kiss" me. What else was there in life? No real responsibility with the Air Force and a job.

What else was there in life? Oh now you remind me to think about the storm. As it turned out I was not allowed to go to the school dance, but I talked with her and she talked with the boy she had to go there with. We had an agreement and I actually got to see her there. Much happened that night to change my life forever, even though I did not understand that it was "GOD" and the "Spirit" leading me towards my walk in life.

A walk that would allow me to be able to identify a "storm" and walk into a "storm" with some understanding. Life was about to change again, and while I did not understand, it was predetermined to allow me to grow. Henry, Carol's step father, stepped into my life and told me that I was restricted from seeing Carol anymore and that he would get me into trouble with the Air Force if I did not listen. He was a contractor at the Air Force Base and said he knew the right people to talk to. That day at school I asked Carol to be engaged with me and she took my ring and told me "no" because she did not want to get me in trouble. What happened? "The Storm." She was told what to do by her step-father.

School was out and Carol moved to Oklahoma City to live with her real father. I waited only four months and began to hitch hike from Moses Lake Washington, to somewhere called Oklahoma City. Little did I know there were mountains in Idaho and cold weather. Dressed in my summer uniform I was in the dark. Then it was called "Grey Hound" and the driver stopped and allowed me to get on the bus. I told him I did not have money for a ticket, however, he allowed me to sleep in the rear of the bus, because it was almost empty.

The trip to Oklahoma City was driven by the desire to find my "girlfriend" and I was determined to do it. Arriving at the address of her father, the first thing I ran into was him working in the garage on a present for his daughter. For over three hours he talked with me about the importance of how to sand the outer surface of a hope chest. I learned the hard way how to again say "yes sir" in the Storm.

Moving closer to reality and life I wanted to get married. I asked questions and got all the difficult answers. Not in Oklahoma, because of the time. Ten days waiting after the paper work, forms, and blood test. What a mess. Then Carol's dad, with someone's help, got the idea that we could go to Texas.

Sure enough, a long drive there, not that four hours is a long time, but in the rush and the do this and do that stuff, Saturday night seemed like forever. Looking back at that moment in time I can now wonder about how different a moment "without" the proper relationship of God's Spirit can cause struggle and difficulty for someone who was living in the flesh.

Needless to say God is still in charge of things, even when we as people in the flesh do not understand the need for HIM in our lives. The marriage took place that night in an Assembly of God Church in Vernon, Texas. Little did I know or even understand that it was an act of proof that the Word of God has truth. The book of Genesis is now the heartbeat of that moment in my life. "In The Beginning."

The rest of the verse and the struggle that Satan used to destroy me and the calling into the WORD remains. While we were so young and innocent we were not even able to be physical in our first night of being husband and wife. The next day we returned to Oklahoma City, and even then I had not truly thought out the time that was to become part of my life in the struggle with my flesh, my body, my soul, and my Spirit.

Little did I know that there was a trip to take. Yes, even the trip back to Oklahoma City, but a trip further and further down the road of life. At that moment I had not even remembered that my leave of 15 days was almost up and that I still needed to return to Moses Lake, Washington. I only had two dollars and 12 cents in my pocket and time did not seem to be important. Why?

Once again the loft seemed to be more welcome.

The Difference Between

Rising on Wednesday morning was seemingly easy for some reason. Questions in my mind were just as simple. What would the day, between 9:00 and 3:45, be like? What would the meeting be like with a Mr. Jason from NY, and an absence of Mr. Masterson on our side mean to me or "The Mountain?"

Walking in deeper snow was the answer, but as I passed the coffee shop I noticed that the dog was not there. That concerned me, or should it? The words of the bible that I remembered was partly a help. "In The Beginning God...." Oh yes, not a dog problem, not a me problem, but a God problem for me to measurably deal with. The walk in the snow seemed to clear my mind. But I did notice there was no music floating in my head. I walked a little more carefully and thought about what? The past. I remember that I was once thinking about serious things before.

With only four days of leave left, I was convinced that borrowing the $93.00, which was a full months pay for me, would be the smart thing to do. Little did I know, that because I had married and could prove it to the A.F. I was soon to be worth $105.00 a month to them. Oh boy, big time coming. Traveling back to Moses Lake on the slow moving bus, I wondered what I should do now and how could I get Carol to where I was stationed. Suddenly life was tuff, and full of ruff, as they always said in the A.F. And I was short of stuff for my tuff and ruff.

No, I still did not know or understand prayer and scripture and God. But HE was leading me in a path. Isaiah 43:16 was in my life, even though I did not know anything about that verse or my life to be in the LORD. The bus moved slowly on toward my military career of three years and thinking about stuff. Now life had changed and I was wondering just where I could go with a wife that I did not even bring home with me.

Time passed, and as I sit here now, Fifty-Five years later thinking back I am still wondering why it is, that I as a young man, did not truly know Jesus Christ as my personal Lord? The flesh of my body and my soul in that flesh was in charge of my life. I did not even realize that what I see now, these years later was even then present to me, but Satan, was still very much in charge of me and my thinking.

The bus pulled into the Moses Lake station and I quickly headed back towards the base. Moses Lake, Washington.

Carol had left her mother and step father, to go to Oklahoma City and now I was here, without my wife, their daughter, and I did not even care if they knew we were married. I did not know or care, and I did not think about telling her mother. That is how I know the physical body and soul can run or control life and the spirit man, called by God's love and Word, is struggling to be born again.

Thinking back to the distant past, I think now about the things that were part of my path to truly get me into a personal relationship with Christ. My friends in the squadron found out that I had gotten married and one of the guys told me that they, he and his wife, would let Carol and I stay with them until we found a place. Right away I needed to talk with my wife and did not even have the $.10 to call her. Life is tuff, and there was another ruff moment. I told the first sergeant my problem and he let me use a loan of a dollar to call my new wife. W.O.W. Things are looking up. When I talked with her, I asked her to come to me on the next bus and I would meet her. "What a day that will be…" are part of the words to a song that I was soon to learn.

A distance of 60 or so miles to Wheeler, Washington was another "storm" in my life, because when Carol called me she was there and not in Moses Lake. Where is Wheeler? What car? How do I get there? Being married was really getting to be hard.

"The Storm" of life is very much present when you begin to realize that the others in the storm are "God" and "Satan" battling for control of life. Even today, I do not remember how I got there, but I did and we, husband and wife, kissed for the first time in a serious way and I began to think about something else. It is also known as "bedtime."

The remaining time at Larson AFB in Washington seems a bit cloudy and yet I do remember getting a job with an oriental family in Moses Lake. We were given the office room to do the job of night time employees and get the late arrivals and the trucker's settled into their rooms for the night. I did the office work and Carol and I had a "home" so to speak.

The hours were adjusted to and the time went by very quickly. I had some ideas about life but they were restricted by my absence of reality and truth. The day to day routine was established until Uncle Sam decided that I needed to be someplace else in the world. Kwajalein seemed to be a long way off in the wrong direction. Not knowing for sure how assignments were chosen or picked was very far behind me in common thinking and the truth was I never gave being separated from Carol any serious thought.

I was told my orders had arrived and I was being shipped to "Turkey" where ever that was. Not caring more about it was my problem in lack of thinking and or planning for the "truth" of life and Satan had a good hold in my living his way. Getting into the assignment overseas again brought us back into family life and Carol's mother helped with relocation. Where is Turkey?

Distance separating me from my wife, and the fact that she was expecting really began to make me hate the Air Force and the truth. A struggle inside made me want to go AWOL. Then my flesh and my Spirit were in a very strong battle. Little did I know that the "walk" of getting truly saved was a pathway that God was showing.

Carol had always been strong yet in all my fleshly thinking, I can truly say she never judged me or condemned me. We were separated by the legalist truth in my career of the Air Force and I expected that this would prove my thinking that I knew more and could do more if I just payed attention to something. The fact is I still was not truly saved or serving the Lord. I was a professional fleshly person with an "act" of hiding from the reality of the WORD of God.

The flight to Turkey seemed like a trip into forever being separated and lost from LOVE. Arrival into Turkey was a life changing experience. Placed on a bus at the commercial airport and herded to a location was a scary reality. Tired and lonely I was back into "The Storm."

Turkey. What a day, or should I say, what a way to separate someone from life? Have you ever wondered why darkness looks so light and bright in a snow storm? Just having experience that in the NOW of my life I wondered just how blind I was allowing myself to get shipped to Turkey? Married and expecting a child. I did not stay with Carol because the Air Force would not allow me to because she was only five months along.

Getting off the bus and standing in front of a 6 or 7 story building I wondered. How could this be the Air Force? As it turned out except for where we actually had to work and where we were placed to sleep, it was the entire Air Force for me for a period of about 21 months.

Glad to get orders to a base called Altus AFB, in Oklahoma. What a day that shall be when my Jesus I shall see, as the song words go.

Returning to the states and my family, Carol and daughter Regina, was a trip toward something I thought was marvelous. Being changed from communication into another career field was a step that I was told was necessary to stay in the Air Force until my discharge.

Oh well, how hard could a clerk job be? Nothing again mattered except LOVE and LIFE with her and our daughter. The Air Force was something that I would just put up with. After all, I knew how to sit pens in a bowling alley, and I knew how to bowl. Being married was not all that tough. So life is not always a "Storm." Or is it?

The storm seemed distant and I was again in charge of my life. Jesus was closer but still in many ways distant from the sound of the marching troops and the possibility of training them for the military combat role in Vietnam.

Two tours as an instructor and then the necessity of getting out of the program led me back into my administrator, AFSC. I took an assignment at the BMT headquarters working as their specialist clerk scheduler. Close to the program but separated by the one-year requirement.

Then it happened again. The Government thinking ahead, said I was wise to request Guam for an assignment because they had a special need for me. It seems like the impact of our force in the effort to help Vietnam was also going to be part of my life. They said I could go there. We, Carol and I, wondered if God was really calling me to go to Vietnam, especially since they were in a war state of trying to kill each other. Prayer, immediately and quickly became another priority in our life.

The day before I was scheduled to leave for Vietnam, we received a called from personnel that I should report back to Lack-land and that my orders to go to Vietnam had been cancelled. Pray was answered.

Back at Lack-land in the clerk mode, so to speak, I was wondering about that Guam assignment that had passed me by. We prayed again about that and continued to work in the administrative field at Lack-land. Once again I received a call to go to personnel and they told me I had another assignment to Vietnam. Yes, it was to a different place there, however, it was still somewhere close to where there was fighting going on. We prayed again, and ask the LORD to help us.

Once again, within a few days of leaving for Vietnam, I received a call that my orders to Vietnam had been changed and that I was being reassigned to go to a job needed on Guam. This time we were amazed because, they told us that the orders had been changed and that I and my family would be leaving soon.

All of us? What a surprise. We had been told in other circles that no dependents were going to the B52 work load on Guam. But somehow, some way, God made a way.

We had a short but pleasant trip to California for the flight to Guam and boarded the plane that day. Carol was feeling ill, and we were troubled with difficulty, however, the trip was necessary. On the plane to Guam we went what I call the Lord's way and in the seating arrangement, our seats were five across the aisle.

Our daughter, then age 10, was sitting beside a man who we did not know but was the supervisor of Government housing on Guam. He played cards with Gina and they got along great during the trip. When he heard what she said, he told me that he could get us a place to stay for a

ATO

while on the Island. When we landed he took care of the details and we ending up in a mobile home settling in.

The next day was a Sunday, and we wanted to find a church. Doing the thinking and the work we located an AOG church pastor's telephone number and he picked us up on the Air Force base. We were finally grounded so to speak. In Guam with a safe job for me, and our family together as a unit. That was and still is a marvelous miracle. To shorten the part of this story, I served and we then returned to the states after a successful tour supporting the Air Force in the Vietnam conflict. Back to Lack-land as a Drill Instructor. "What a day that will be…"as the song goes.

Back at Lackland AFB, we had a second tour as MTI's assignment and we were nearing the end of my Air Force career. I only had 11 months to go for full retirement and I received another call, from personnel saying that there was an open assignment on Guam and if I wanted to go there again I would have to re-enlist to fulfill the time requirement. Praise the Lord. I was about to go over 20 years of service and get paid for going to Guam again. Now my family had aged and my second child, James did not want to go. His grandmother said she would keep him in Dallas and we could travel without him. So be it? Not now, but then it seemed like a good idea.

The second tour on Guam was also joint and we arrived and accepted my new assignment with the understanding that I could remain on Guam until I was eligible to retire and pick my base of choice to return to the United States. That was a really good deal, so to speak. When the tour was up we were getting close to retirement, however, Regina and our pastor's son were doing some serious dating and a few days before leaving Mark announced that they wanted to be married.

Carol and I said, not no but never because we were leaving Guam shortly. We shipped Regina back early and we thought that would fix her problem with a "boyfriend." The day after the flight she left on Mark came to the house and snapped enough money on the table to fly her back to Guam so that they could be married. We began to rethink and plan. We left Guam for a base in Louisiana for my retirement assignment. Regina was in Dallas getting ready to go back to Guam and I was trying to figure out what I should be doing now. Where is God anyway?

Once again, walking past the coffee shop I noticed that Love was not under the window. Where was Mr. Masterson? Why did he not want to come to the meeting?

Unsettled

Generally speaking, Wednesday was an average day, and the meeting was not until 3:00 pm which left one hour of time to say what needed to be said. As I entered the office I said to Carol, "Please come in. I have a couple of items."

We have a 3:00 with Mr. Jason form N.Y. Setup the conference room with audio and video in case we need it and schedule Mr. Allen from Legal to be there and invite one of the staff from contractors to be there also. No cookies and ice cream. You and your notebook please. If you have a private number for Mr. Masterson, please call it and tell him that he is invited to attend.

Wanting to re-think my thoughts, about what, where, when, and if, my mind began to drift again.

Why do I feel so unsettled? Where is HE when I need HIM? Such is life in real time. Once again my past entered into the room.

The officer I was assigned to was the Chief of Personnel at the base. He told me that I was not really there to work but to get ready for retirement. He allowed me to drive the 97 miles to our home place in East Texas, as long as

I checked in once a week. Home alone so to speak with retirement scheduled in just a few more months. What now? A Garden? A place to fish? But, also, or youngest son still under our watchful eye. What to do now?

Retirement so to speak, was there without understanding and without purpose or peace of mind. We were at a safe haven of choice, with obligations considered and without the big bucks of the previous life, but something I thought was where I should be. Guess that stuff is not important when you do not measure the need for stuff in the proper time. In either case I was in a period of "running away from home" in my own way of saving face.

Our son Bryan was hit by a car on the main road coming from Chandler to the lake and we had to go through what was an emergency for his life. Much happened that was not preplanned or needed yet we were able to get on with all the stuff.

Checking in years later, with stuff on my mind. Cannot always remember the day in my past when I should begin to re-enter this story of my life. Time is so precious now and I am guilty of not getting into the right mode, or right place, in my busy life. There is nothing understandable about this in a way, because I have to finish the book, so to speak, and that is something that I do not plan on doing right now.

It appears that I am about to be living in the "retired world" of life and stuck in it also. What does that do to my life story? That is a good question. Because, I am still here, at the age of 75, with a broken or dented brain of 8 years with that thing called encephalitis. What should I do with this story, or where should I go in the next part of life? That is the question that I cannot answer knowingly at this time. Part of me wants to close this and be done with it. Part of me wants to wait and see, and part of me is as you might read, now confused.

What is encephalitis? That is what we were told happened to me eight years ago.

Because of it I have worked on getting "back" to what was, or what should be me. That is where this document came into existence from and where this document must remain for a period of time also known as life. Example: Looking for the previous edition to "The Pond" for the original until this year copy.

The scripture does say: This know also, that in the last days, perilous times shall come. 2 Tim 3:1. The problem with encephalitis was and still is doing something with the current part of life, but trying to remember the past part of life to accomplish it.

Military retirement left two years of civilian life which was not correctly planned for. Locating a new way of life and getting back into that was difficult, but done, and the Civil Service career is part of that life.

The meeting scheduled for today was an important part of needing to remember other parts of my past, but not limiting myself to that time. The meeting would still be part of life.

What Time Is It?

No Mr. Masterson at the coffee shop and no Love waiting there. Perhaps I just figured out why the bible has so much to mention on the subject of prayer. I did not know exactly how, or why, but I did say "God Help Me."

Turning back toward the office, I looked at my watch and noted that there was a very impressive car pulling to the front door. The driver helped two gentlemen out and then pulled the car away to the parking lot. I said "Excuse me, I am Mr. Sherman. Are you Mr. Jason?" He said "yes I am and this is an interesting place to meet. I can see the Mountain very clearly."

Entering the door, I notified the office we were going directly to wing eight, and the conference room. "Please inform the others to meet us." As we settled in, I said once again quietly to myself, "God Help Me."

Without further introduction of staff and people gathering, Mr. Jason said "We have come to climb the mountain. We are here to tell you of some things that are important. We know that because of the state and business law you all have a 30 day formal response time to our information. Take all of that time if required" He then ask the person with him to speak.

"Hello, my name is Mr. Wilson, spokesperson for ABC. I am here to tell you that we want to climb the mountain and tell everyone that we care. That is the quickest way I can explain ABC. Always Be Correct is here to present to every person, every family, every identity, a free offer of a month's supply of water and food. No strings attached, other than for you to as a receiver, say you want to be part of ABC."

"Using the facilities of "The Mountain" we want to import the product and deliver the product to everyone in the city, the county, and the state. Thank You."

Silence filled the room. I looked at Mr. Jason, Mr. Allen, and then Carol as I asked the question. "Does the 30 days included weekends or are they our business days.? They said, pick or choose either one, that is fine. Speaking to our legal and to Mr. Allan face to face, I said "draw it up and we will look at it."

I closed the meeting with an idea. I asked them if someone would like to pray. Mr. Jason said he would and then said "In the Beginning God Created the Heaves and the Earth, help us Lord to be part of that beginning. Amen."

I thanked everyone for their time as we stood to walk out. Our visitors said they would be in touch and if we had questions feel free to contact them. There I remembered something I had written earlier in the time pasted. It had to do with time in a different way and it was written in my pen name writer "Hislerim"

T -Truths

I-Immediate

M-Measurable

E-Eternity

Thinking about the value of time or the reason for time and that is measurable is not the problem. How often have we heard "next time" or "perhaps later?" The thought process some evidence of something was to remember time and its importance. Getting back to "My Life" as a document that was written in and about time was now enforced again.

Truthfully Speaking

The rest of the week would perhaps be a turning point. I asked Carol to inform the entire staff, that we would have a Friday 1:00 pm meeting and to bring their notebooks. All personnel, no exceptions including birthday people.

I was looking forward to the weekend, the mountain, the snow and the purpose of planning for a future of time. Wondering about what happened because Mr. Masterson could have attended the meeting but did not.

Friday night and what? Should I learn? The past in my life has been and continues to be very strongly motivated. Yet I struggle with the concern that I am not sure. Dealing with the past, and placing it properly into the future as needed or desired, especially as now, is part of the difficulty. The winter weather, on the mountain, a new path or plan that sounds great, but causes wonder and the need for information. I need the truth.

Then I remembered the scripture that had been such an interesting part of this struggle. I searched my bible at the loft and looked up the passage that I was thinking about. John 8:32, now easily remembered, but not necessarily understood. I had accepted the fact that much more than a single verse was correct. There were fifty-nine verses in chapter eight of the book of John. I reread the entire chapter and sat without prayer and thought of what it said.

What is truth in any matter under consideration? What is truth in things, apparently to God verses, duty to man in life? What is truth in the subject of NY wanting to be in or on the mountain? Where was or where is Mr. Masterson? What is my concern? Once again the idea or force of thinking brought me to the concept of prayer.

Saying out loud "God that man said 'In The Beginning, God Created the Heavens and the Earth', Lord, help us to understand." I remembered that part of the meeting. Now what part did God, or I or the absence of Mr. Masterson become in all of that "beginning?"

Then I decided to call my wife, Carol, and ask her to pray about the decisions I had to make. I was here, she was there, and if anything I remembered that she knew more about prayer than I did. The time I had spent was nearing the end of the promise that I had made to her about being gone and the time of the decision to approach something known as ABC and the wonder of the mountain. What was next? Where was Mr. Masterson? Why did I want to know more about what he thought?

I remembered something I had learned in school about bible numbers. Subtracting the two from the number eight left the number six. Six was the number of man. Adding the eight and the two together, was the number 10. Subtracting the zero from the one in 10 left the number one. Who or what was the number one in the decisions that I would be making in the next year of life if I stayed at the mountain? If I did not have Mr.

Masterson to tell me what to do? If I entered into a contract with Mr. Jason in a job or a part of business which would be known as About Being Correct?

Then I remembered that was not the original name I had heard. What was ABC in New York that I remembered. I called my thinking into reality and remembered it was A = Always B=Be C=Christian. Why did they now want to change the name to something different? Prayer?

The mountain had a climbing path that was easy and it had a climbing path that was nearly impossible. What did that have to do with ABC and what did it have to do with now?

Relocation from Oklahoma to "The Mountain" would be interesting and for whatever reason I did not even think how difficult it might be. Let's just do it. The crew settled into the conference room and the buzzer on the desk buzzed and reminded me that was where I was supposed to be. Entering into that room, without knowing why or how, Mr. Masterson was there.

Welcome to the real world of "The Mountain." Let's talk about the climb up during the winter season of time. I ask the staff to be seated and noted that Mr. Masterson was in a seat that could see out the window. I also saw that he was looking at the Mountain.

As quickly as I could I told them about the ABC meeting and the idea that they wanted to open up a starting program to give everyone in the city and the state a free one time offer of water and food for a month. No questions or requirements, other than to ask the question about being able to understand About Being Correct or ABC for short.

Then I asked the legal team to do a background study on ABC start to finish, in its original location and purpose. I asked the others to provide a list of what it meant to be given a month's supply of water and food free. The only thing they would be required to do is promote ABC. Told the staff it was late but to take the rest of Friday off and be prepared for a wonderful, perhaps confusing Monday. I did mention that each branch would have one of our people on the team of ABC and they would be required to document the day by day, week by week, month by month activity to hold for documentation of the next decision that had to be made at the end of a year.

Knowing the "truth" of the "time" would either give us a reason for LOVE of what we were known for or it would tell us that it was not truly LOVE. Mr. Masterson asked if he could speak to the group.

"Without going into a great deal of information at this time it is part of a decision that I have struggled with since the "Mountain" started reducing in both size and business. We are "The Mountain." That was the original dream and that was why I stopped the first day and made the climb. Today I feel like I am at one of the places on the difficult size of the mountain, facing the decision to either turn left or right. Wondering why Left seems better than Right. The only measurement I have to know for sure is The Word of God and the Truth. Pray and enjoy your weekend. Thank you."

Real Life On the Mountain

Walking home from the meeting and from the week, I had a flash of time which returned to me without permission.

That is what I am referring to when I say that "My Life" as a book, or even as a place of interest in something that troubles me.

Arriving in Oklahoma from the 21 hour plus air trip from Guam was a relief of sorts. Expecting that it would be acceptable to just drop in on Carol's father without too much notification was somewhat stupid to say the least.

Summer time in Oklahoma with the temperatures in the upper 90s plus was interesting because of the climate differences from Guam. One day at a time, the song says and that is exactly the way I was living. Without too much time, I began again to wonder why I left a secure Government job to come back to nothing. Except to be in the "states" as we used to say in the old days.

Several weeks into the return, I began a look at the back pages of the daily Oklahoman for something. The answer to your question is yes, I was doing it without much thought of God and or HIS word. Never the less, there was some confidence in me that made me think that I could do something. The ad for Churches Fried Chicken managers looked real good and surprisingly they accepted my first call. Back to work with approximately a 15 to 20 minutes' drive and a 10-hour day I was once again able to tell Carol to come home.

For whatever reason I had not thought about getting back into Civil Service. Having completed 22 weeks of training in to how to fry chicken and get rid of it within 12 to 15 minutes was my life.

One day, I found myself at Tinker Air Force Base, Civilian Personnel building filling out a possible job application. That day was a day of stupid training in Civil Service. Many people were there with me that day, and as the day continued I noticed at the lunch hour that many of them left and did not come back in. I waited and I waited and at 4:30 that afternoon, a voice started calling names. No one was in the room beside the clerk at the counter and me. When he called my name "SHERMAN", I said here.

He told me to have a seat and sign a form. After that he said, I will see you at 7:30 tomorrow morning here. I left without even knowing his name. Back the next day. At 7:00 I waited and at 9:30 he called me into the other room. Gave me paper work to fill out and told me a physical would be required. Here we go again, and all I could think about was "Welcome to Civil Service."

It turned out that I was being hired to fill a vacant GS-3 slot in the Computer Branch. Whatever that was I had re-entered civil service and the chicken power place lost.

Going into work on the first official day I was told to go to building 3001, room 204 and wait. I found the longest building—3001—on Tinker and went to the second story of the building and found room 204. The room was empty, with no desk, no telephones, no people and I stood in the door way waiting for something to happen. Monday, Tuesday, Wednesday, Thursday, and Friday of the first week before I got somewhat stupidly angry. I had not seen the man that hired me, nor had I seen anyone else so I decided this was a great way to get paid for doing nothing except to stand in an empty room in a big building. Wait until next Monday.

The following Monday I saw a person about three sections down from the room I was supposed to be at and I asked if they knew anything about a new computer group that was supposed to work there. He said he had heard about it but did not know much more, that I should ask the security people down stairs if they knew anything. Thinking about that made me want to quit work and go back to the chicken job. I found an empty room that had a chair and I moved it to my 204 room and sat down again. Waiting and wondering about why this was supposed to be called by a name I did not even realize.

So I wandered the building until I found the main computer room location, and started asking questions about who, what, when, why and where. It was surprising to find so many people that did not know anything about a broadband LAN project, or base wide computer installation.

That day, I saw the guy that hired me and I forced my way into his area. I asked him where was I supposed to be working. He asked me if I knew how to mount tapes on main frames and I said "huh!"

The next week was the civil service pay day and I got a check and decided that I was working in the right place, with the right job in building 3001, room 204.

Actually, a man ran into me and said "Oh, there you are" and I asked for his name. He explained that he had been told I was hired, but he could not understand why I had not reported for work. Handing me a machine run listing of information, approximately 60 pages long, he said, "let's get started."

Looking at the list, he said we would use it to locate the requirements for the new cable plan layout and the inventory prospective for computers at Tinker Air Force Base. Now, I had something to think about and go do. WOW actually WOW, it was a 60 plus page list of information. Building #1 was our first stop.

Counting days, not that it should be done, but thought of as a way to remember the use of time in life, is difficult when age is a factor.

Looking back at the past, what might be or perhaps was important, is the fun part of difficulty. Civil Service in the retirement age of returning to the U.S. After time of being in the overseas civil service world, was quite a shock to say the least. Not understanding why or how civil service is "locked" into its tradition, but knowing now, several years later that it is locked in a misguided idea of career planning is part of my problem.

Thinking about a time that will happen without knowing when that time is supposed to be is difficult when you are writing a book about the life past. Thinking ahead is easier than remembering the past.

Like watching a screen saver on a note book computer while you are typing in a journal of time. Each rock in the back yard pond was required, needed, during the time of design, yet the design was not necessarily pre-thought for purpose. Even today, with winter creeping up, the design of the pond needs consideration. Why is that important?

Only the winter weather and time will tell because of the multiple types of fish in the pond and the reason for each purchase. Back for a few minutes in time. Getting into the process of leaving the other place, space, time, and coming into this world is what I am referring to.

My life, in the process of staying on Guam for a civil service job, with reference to feeling secure, and dropping it at a moment's notice and returning to the states for an idea of helping Carol feel secure, was my issue. Back here, the civil service cycle opened up again and I entered into a new world of security with the concept of computers and networks as the basis for why I existed.

Looking at the calendar, the 24th of October was the next day and my biggest concern for the moment was surprising my wife with a breakfast in bed—one that was different than any of the previous ones. When you think about that, one Saturday a month, one breakfast each time with the idea of proving my love is something to write about also.

Perhaps I can add a paragraph later on that subject. The music on i-Tunes is not necessarily the motivation but the screen saver on the other CPU reminds me of the hard work the back yard pond has been. In some ways it is amazing and in other ways I have to ask myself why? When the age of time gets my focus then I wonder how long before it will be completely finished and something to marvel over.

Leaving Guam and the security of Civil Service was easy, without too much consideration, but coming back into security was a different matter. God provided the pathway and the security of the next few years that I had responsibility for and actually retired with 22 years, six months and one day of time.

Now each day is not going to be part of this story but there were a few days in that process that showed how difficult it was to work for a living doing something the government wants, but does not have the slightest idea of why, when, where, or how to do it and save the tax payer their money. In other words, it is spend, spend, spend, and hope that you buy something that can be used somewhere, someday.

Retirement from the civil service process actually came at a difficult time because of the changes being made by Uncle Sam in their thinking about tomorrow, and not too concerned that the mistakes they made in the past were now causing a few hundred to retire. So I left, with another blanket of security, yet unsure of what or why the next day was going to bring. Being retired is a difficult term if you as an individual have no idea of what that really and truly is. The house payment, the insurance to adequately cover it and the cars, the food, the utilities are all still part of life. Why retire? Or why, are you, at that time not prepared to be there?

All of that happened and since I am here now, looking back at 2000 it has been almost 15 years and things are secure or somewhat better. House is paid for, car is paid for, the insurance is once every six months for a lot more than I want to pay, and food is necessarily getting to be a little better, with a little less.

That does not change the work on 5 acres, the grass to mow in the spring and early summer and the fact that I can hit a golf ball on any part of it, toward any flag, in any weather, and fish at the big pond while I am looking for a golf ball that was lost. What day of the week is it? Who is really too concerned about that when you can honestly say it is my life, my pond, and most of all it is understandably under God's control.

The thinking was clear, because it was like I stood on top of the mountain and someone was speaking clearly to me saying "This is life, and you have lived it." Now deal with reality and remember that I am God, and that changes not.

Learn about time and the truth, but do it in Love. The scripture has so much to say about love. Brotherly kindness in or of itself is a life time of learning and I had until Monday to get started in "The Mountain" blending with "The ABC," as a Moral Ideal, or as Actual Between the two identities, or just in starting a new way of living. From a part time job, to a full time job or as we said in the military world "get out and get a job." Life was not here. Thinking it through was easier because of the time that had passed.

The strength that I received when Mr. Masterson was visible. The fact that there was in fact his bible in the office that he had placed me with. Time, Truth and Love had started a mending in my life of retirement and the next day or so I would be hearing from Carol, my wife, saying what I needed to know. Having to stay or go from here would be a leading of God's Spirit in each of the areas. The Time, The Truth and The Love.

Always wondering about the next step, or thinking about something that is slightly beyond my reach is a struggle. Building the bridge between the pages that have been completed and the next part of this writing is a path that is choosable, yet concerning. Life goes on so to speak and this is a place to change. That is why I want to use the Word and look at a different place. Picking the book of Exodus was within reason, even though parts of my thinking wanted to jump to revelations. Of course.

Consideration for an Exodus when in fact there was always a path to follow, and a place to be within reason, was something that has happened. Knowing the path to take from here to there, or understanding the Exodus was the next step. What little I knew about this book in the bible could fill multiple pages of any writing and that is only a slight exertion. Where it is in the bible of course is easy to know, because it is close to my love of Genesis, but that is not why I started thinking about it. Moving forward, since the damage to my body was done, was necessary. Wanting to do it during the rain storm, or the ice storm, is the problem with my thinking.

During the process of wondering why, or thinking about the steps to take, I remembered the climbs that I have made and will continue to make on the mountain. There is a place on the path where you see that point. There is a choice between the "left path" and the "right path." That point on the mountain reminds me.

"The steps of a good man are ordered by the LORD: and he delighted in his way." Psalms 37:23. There is or could be a few ways to thinking about that verse. Perhaps it is because the word "steps" is within it. Perhaps it is the concept of "good man" being ordered by the LORD. But the climb on the mountain has always been upward, with the choice of changing to downward. So Be It.

Leaving The Time of Yesterday

Exodus, or going out, was a good way to say, do you want to turn left or do you want to turn right? The weather was cold and the mountain seemed to be longing to be left alone. Why did I feel so strongly about that? The meeting with the new people was not scheduled until next month, and they would only have 5 or 7 initial people coming. What was the truth of reason behind the plant accepting this project?

Always Be Correct sounded good, but what happened to Always Be Christian? That stuck inside me like a bear growl. For some reason unsettled was insufficient to the feeling that I had over the idea. Yet something inside made me feel required to go through the process of evaluation based on the findings of our staff.

Calling Mr. Jason, I requested an early shipment of both a gallon of the water and a full case of the food that would be issued. I told him we would be testing and or building advertisement around the products and wanted to see firsthand what we were about to take into consideration. Expecting an argument, Mr. Jason, said "O.K. We will air ship it tomorrow."

Now I was really lost or not clearly thinking about why, or what I just did. Was I truly leaving the old place and did I know what it meant to wonder in the desert of life? For some reason I felt like we had had a good year, for the most part, and also I felt like something in the past was missing, or that I did not understand the truth of what Mr. Masterson had said. We were to enjoy the weekend.

Knowing Saturday was a day of relaxation, I fully intended to climb the mountain to the first place where there was a joint or stopping place where I was forced to turn either left or right. That would be the place that I could find an answer.

Starting the climb that morning was interesting because I had dressed differently and expecting very cold weather along the path I had an extra pair of socks on. My clothes were warm but I had not taken into consideration the very strong wind, blowing or even perhaps gusting, from what felt like the top of the mountain. We may find it perplexing to note that there were other places in life that faced the same environment.

Not very well studied up, I could not quote passages in the bible, but I did remember the tone of Mr. Masterson's voice and his concern that we were going through a struggle or battle and so was this climb looking for a place that I must choose either a left or right turn. Why could I not find it? It was there somewhere in the past. People remember things from the past, and they think of them from a view point of wanting that now. Was I still in Egypt, or had I taken my first steps into the charge and stubbornness of the plan of God for our lives, and what was my expectation?

Why did the people in the book of the bible, also known as Exodus, have their problems? There is something we know when we look at it, because there is a problem with the fact that we did something and then we notice it. What does the job, the building, the mountain, and the new ABC Company add on have to do with any of that?

Where is Mr. Masterson? When I cannot find an answer of my understanding and I want help I always think of him. Perhaps I should go back to what he said. Learn about time and the truth, but do it in love. What is time, what is truth and where do I show or know I am doing it, that is in time, and in truth, with love.

Always with the newness of looking ahead, or perhaps being aware of the wind touching me as if to say "I am with you" or perhaps it was just the fact that light, the beauty of blue, the sound of now all around made me wonder more about being closer to the Word.

Yes, there is more to understand than the words "In The Beginning God. . . . . . "

Getting Started in Reality

Beginning to enter into the concept that "The Mountain" was or perhaps could be seen as changing from its origination, caused me to climb harder, and higher, even while the weather was so cold. Taking the approach that I was at the front office level of responsibility, instead of shipping, caused me to want to be better and within my first year of position I needed to understand that time and opportunity had relocated me into existence. I actually had a new life.

This life, however, was certainly able to upside things. Carol had arrived and we settled into our new apartment life and within reason the responsibility of the old life was erased. I had a peaceful placement into the power or the position of life, yet I stood at a distance from all of the issues that were still in front of me.

Leaving the old life of struggle for a new life of consideration was the reason and purpose. Hopefully, the new products would arrive early in the week and we could evaluate them from an outsider's view point.

Returning to work on Monday, I immediately had the office staffer tell me if new mail had been received. He said not anything important, just a couple of boxes of stuff he had not examined. I ask him not to be offended, but I wanted to see what they were.

Plain brown wrappers are labels of warning to protect the content. Wondering if the box was difficult to open or heavy I ask him to quickly show me the content. He said "Boss, that's nothing to be concerned about. I do this for a pay check."

First box was a plastic gallon of water, with stuffing around the container and he lifted it out and said "It's water?" Quickly as I could, taking it away from his grip I said "call the staff, it is here."

The second box was approximately two sizes bigger yet lighter in weight. Opening it was almost fun.

The individual containers were wrapped separately and looked similar in shape and size. Simple labels, but appeared to be a foreign language. Oh now what? "Take it all to the conference room and call the staff together there."

What next? It was only 9:10 am. Reaching for the telephone, I asked Carol to connect me to Mr. Jason. If he is not there, ask anyone there that can answer the question; "What language are these labels?"

Born early into misunderstanding issues that even I was surprised with. Upset with life as the stuff sat on the table of the conference room was perhaps a difficult way of looking at something that I thought should be different. Wanting Mr. Masterson was not wrong, was it?

Talking with legal, I said evaluation of labels is your job. A representative of each branch will take the product boxes apart, one at a time and evaluate the content by experimentation of proof. What is it? What does it taste like? Why is it discussed in words that cannot be understood?

What day of the week is this? Call my wife and explain that I will not be home for lunch and perhaps I might be late for supper. I wanted to know more about what was in the box and why did it look different? What is going to be re-packaged?

When and if the "Mountain" had to be climbed I wanted to be the one leading the group up.

Telling the office staff to enjoy their lunch period, I walked again to the coffee shop praying that I would find Mr. Masterson. He was not there.

Then walking back, I thought of the book of the bible called Exodus. If I remembered correctly the nation of Israel was mighty and noteworthy and was something to be secure in. Then I felt peace inside and related to the fact that perhaps I could take a short lunch break in the office and read some of what was part of the life of the people when they were being afflicted by the Egyptians and there was a ruling force trying to control their life.

The Angle of Distance All Around

I neared what seemed to be the top of the mountain, which ended up to be a level area and several miles across. Remembering that I was getting started in a new day was almost forgotten until I saw, once again, the two birds circling far above me.

Keeping the "Mountain" was not just as easy as looking out the window where the mountain was visible. Today, for example, the snow and the wind almost prevented visibility of the mountain and keeping the concept that every decision would be a decision that kept the surrounding mountain intact was necessarily the visible concept.

Looking around at the building we worked in, the color of the paint, the door swinging right or left, the windows in or outside, was a visible wonder. What appeared was in some ways a flame of warning or distance of thinking. Looking at the inside of the building, the history, the existing staff. What about looking at the building outside?

Certainly I had not asked the inner staff to evaluate the way I looked at things. So I called Carol into the office an asked her to post a picture and a statement on the hallway bulletin board: "Visualize the Boss." Submit your ideas on why and how he must change. A three-man group will select the winner who will be rewarded with a paid dinner at a local restaurant of their choice. Turn around and look at the boss with a view that you want to look through because of "Time, Truth and Love."

Back to the concept of the change that was expected to start soon. Why had they not called explaining the labeling of the containers? Perhaps it was their test of our ability to get in, or get out. Why was it interesting to wonder about?

There was a verse in the bible I tried to remember. Seek ye first? Where was it? What did I wonder about the whole business concept, when I was in shipping as a new hire just a little over a year ago and today I was in the founder's office sitting at his desk?

Something said to me "What did Moses think about?" It seems clear now that was why Mr. Masterson had said look at the bible I left in the office. Oh no, where is what I need to find? Oh yes there is an index. What should I be looking for? Why did I always think of Mr. Masterson instead of the bible? Was I walking in what the idea of Exodus is? Escaping?

Identification of the truth seemed to be my greatest desire, yet I had forgotten there was time to begin with. I did wake up today, I did once again look for Love, remembering her with thinking clearly, and then I did remember that my wife had plans for that day also. Moreover, I said that I did not follow the Word exactly. From the day that I had climbed the mountain nearly the first time, the path around it came into my way of thinking.

Now something reminded me that I could see things that appeared to be a problem, in a different way, if I clearly wanted to see the element of Love in the Time and the Truth. Listening to the staff members, and asking if what they were saying was part of God's plan, and then, if I did not know, look for the answer in the Word. Do not get too upset if you do not always stop and look for Mr. Mr...What's his name?

On the intercom, I asked Carol if Mr. Jason had called. Had she heard anything from ABC? Why if they said the name ABC was "Always Be Correct" or "Always Be Christian" did they not return my call? Then it hit me again, there was another scripture I could not find in my memory. "Judge not less ye be judged." Where did that come from?

Legal, the labels on the boxes and the labels on the products are your responsibility. Do not forget to scan the item with our shipping department and see what labels our equipment will print. Climbing-in this mountain climb was in some ways a different kind of climb, because at least I was inside a building and not on the side of a snow layered mountain.

What kind of taste test do we want to do? Get a rep from each branch in and let's play a game. Have them blindfold themselves, let someone else pick a product without telling them which meal box it is from and let them guess about the product. Keep notes. Remember, we may be required to re-produce this stuff in a different way. Like getting a different kind of dictionary if you know what I mean. Why did I say that? Why did I not say it like one of the other translations of the bible? KJV, NIV, Amplified? This was a test in ways that I had not considered, or concerned myself with. The understanding of the truth was not at question, but knowing the truth was something that I seemed to have misunderstood.

Centered in Security

Wondering why the separation from Mr. Jason and Mr. Masterson was troubling me was not as difficult in some ways as being away from the security of my relationship with my wife during my business day. Without knowing for sure why, I trusted my wife's thinking about things and wanted to be able to ask her. I could not just hire her into the building and call her something, but the idea was defining because of the mountain.

Separation from her was difficult on any given business day, but more so on specific situation days because I recognized her ability to clarify my thinking.

Looking toward the office and the staff, immediately I was impacted by the decision to fill the empty wing with new people, a new business idea, and the impact that it could have on the company. What would the staff say if I asked them today, to decide today, if we should go ahead or decline the offer?

How long shall I take counsel in my soul, having sorrow in my heart daily? How long shall mine enemy be exalted over me? Quoted from Psalms 13 verse 2. How long do we labor at reaching an idea before we decide?

Working in the front office, instead of working in the shipping department, was significant and different because of the expectation.

Teaching myself to be different was like remembering the day I climbed the mountain and found the dog. That is a special day and one that pleases my way of remembering. Where is the dog and the owner? Why can't he sit in the office I am sitting in?

Carol on the intercom said "Mr. Jason is on line 1." Oh what now? "Sir, I said, we have received the shipment of both the water and the second box of meals. My question was intended to be ask, why is the product labeled as is? Mr. Jason said, "Not to worry, your staff and ours will be changing it when we start." My next question was one of interest.

"When do your first people arrive for the test and the evaluation stage of the product and the distribution plan for our location? It was not my intention to be bossy but there can only be a single point of reasoning. I want to know the truth from the get go."

Mr. Jason said "Thank you for being straight forward we will be in touch again soon." He hung up very quickly.

On the intercom, I clicked over to legal and said: "Find out anything significant? What did you find out about the ABC Company in New York?"

And the LORD said unto him, what is that in thine hand? And he said, A rod. Thinking out loud or wondering why Exodus 4 came into my thinking process. The process of this project was struggling with my flesh—or perhaps with my spirit. The effort to keep everything focused into a proper sense of reality that the business we called "The Mountain." Then I remembered that Moses was called out or call while he was on the mountain. *And Moses went up unto God, and the LORD called unto him out of the mountain, saying, thus shalt thou say to the house of Jacob, and tell the children of Israel.* The bible in the window of my office. There again was an answer from the search, and finding it was so simple. Thank you, Mr. Masterson for leaving the bible here.

Now I could go back to the book with the confidence that the book had an answer for everything. "In the Beginning." Why did I believe that? Because there were two covers on this book and the first one and the last one made me want more of what was in between.

A Rod to Receive By

Belief in something sufficient, within reason, if you do not know for sure why you are interested is the place I found myself. I was wondering about the significance of the total process. Then the factor that they, that is the people from the Jason side of the process, would be here shortly. Being retired military and retired civil service caused me to wonder about the chain of command and or the authority in a civilian business world. Was I truly the boss?

Calling Carol to the office, I asked her if anyone had put anything into the suggestion box about me. She said that it was in the hallway and the rules were to empty it every third Friday. That was still two days away. Why did I feel so anxious?

What type of test could I give myself to find out if I did believe in my ability to lead the path up the mountain? Walking the hallway, I went to the shipping department to see why or if they had interviewed anyone for the opening in that branch. Looking at the mountain from that wing was amazing. The snow seems to be leaving. Spring was in the air—but several weeks from officially being there.

Looking back at the time of Love being found and the test that I had for helping her get her foot free was an escape in facing the unfilled position in shipping. Why did my being the previously employee handy man bother me?

Remembering finding Love and helping her seemed to give me peace of mind, but then I wondered why it took several weeks to find the owner who was also the president of the place I worked at? Why and when would difficulty become easier?

The intercom buzzed and Carol said it was NY calling about a question they had. Picking up the telephone I said "how can we be of service?" They wanted to know if they could have 3 to 5 people on the next flight out of New York to come and setup for the beginning of the walk through.

What is a walk through? He said, you will enjoy being part of our walk through. Next week OK with you?

Now the mountain snow seemed to be melting too fast, and I was hoping for a later freeze or new snow fall. The message of the reason was, I wall still unsettled as to the reason why we were part of what was called the "mountain" processing stuff that was to be given free, by ABC.

I notified the staff to set up an office space in the West Wing and call it or label it "Mountain – ABC." Paint the walls a combination of "red, white and blue" and put a flag in the room. Have the room ready by Tuesday of next week,

So I found out that and Moses said unto the LORD, O my Lord, I am not eloquent, neither heretofore, nor since thou hast spoken unto thy servant: but I am slow of speech, and of a slow tongue. But, then that was in the book. Oh well, if I remember Mr. Masterson did say to read it.

Remembering that I was in the building also known as the "Mountain" and that there was a real one visible from all the windows on the east side of the building and that Mr. Masterson was the owner of Love and related to me in a 55% of the building, and company name, I was OK with someone from Mr. Jason's end coming to the office.

How to greet them? Check the weather in NY and see if they were coming to better or worse weather and welcome anyway.

I told Carol to call my Carol and ask the question: Can I plant a garden this coming spring? That should make everyone in the building wonder if I knew what I was doing? In either case the mountain was still standing, and even though we had a mild winter, the possible rain and storms of spring would make things interesting.

Taking time to stop and wonder, I picked up the bible in the office and opened it to the book of Exodus. Exodus 4:11 And the LORD said unto him, Who hath made man's mouth? or who maketh the dumb, or deaf, or the seeing, or the blind? have not I the LORD?

How Big Is a Brick?

The plane touched down and taxied in to the private parking area slow but sure. The noise from the very visible private jet was softened. As it parked, the center ladder dropped and Mr. Jason stepped out followed by Sue, Peter and Bob. A foursome? Why? Mr. Jason started down the steps and looked back at the pilot and said three to four days. Enjoy it on the mountain.

Mr. Jason said, Hi Sherman, we will settle in and I will have the crew meet this part of the staff tomorrow at your building. We have reservations at the Sheridan and transportation fixed. We will see you tomorrow.

Thinking that perhaps Mr. Jason had already climbed the mountain in NY, I thanked him and told my group to go back to the office and wait for what I expected to be some sort of difficult thinking meeting tomorrow at 9:00 am.

Speaking to legal on the way back I ask them to have the list of the product we wanted named ready. Make three choices with the least liked on the top of the list, the best liked on the bottom of our list, and the other one in the middle. We have done that. Do you want the copy now?

Sure I said. He replayed ABC, right? I said right. "Always be Cabbage Lettuce, Always be Carefully Chosen, and Always be Concerned Wisely. What do you think boss?"

Weird choices. But let's say they pick the lettuce one. We will use that as a disclaimer and tell them we are bowing out of the entire project.

Remembering the scripture I had read about Moses and Aaron going into Pharaoh and asking to let the people go, I said, see you all at 1:00 pm in the conference room.

At exactly 1:00 pm the crew of four pulled up in the service they used and I could tell that Sue was Mr. Jason's contact with the public. She was engaged even though they stepped out of the van. Peter and Bob were on the left and right side of Mr. Jason.

Mr. Jason said "Let's get it done. We are a team. We do not want to stop the process from getting started the first of this coming year. We are a team and we want to show and prove that to the city, the community, and most of all, to the mountain."

No sooner in the conference room and Mr. Jason said "have you picked the name for the product that will be disbursed from this location?" We gave him the list. He said, "I like your number three better than the other two. 'Always Be Concerned Wisely.' It marries the ABC concept of need. Why did you pick that one?" I replied, "Because of the major issue with your company name ABC. It sort of blends into the concept of organization and concept of team desire."

Then Mr. Jason said "That's completely the reason we came. Do you have any question about taking the label

148

to the next processing step? The work load will be done by our department in NY and we will forward the program to your system next week on Monday or Tuesday. Peter and Bob will stay for a week or 10 days to talk with you."

"Challenge your thinking about product distribution and public awareness. We will need that as soon as the labels are available to print. Other than that, Sue and I will head back in the morning and before we leave, I want to climb part of the mountain, regardless of the weather. See you soon." They quickly left and Peter and Bob stood and said, "We will be in contact, boss?"

Taking Peter and Bob to their office area, I said, "The desk, copy machine, and internet connection are all up and ready. Make sure you CC the front office on all communication with NY and remember that the office hours are from 8 to 4 or 9 to 5 which ever, both of you want but one will be on each shift."

How big is a brick? Not sure but it was getting heavy.

Higher or Lower, That Is the Question

Wanting to divide the land or the work, was not the issue with me, but keeping track of certain areas of interest so that when Mr. Masterson was part of the issue, he would understand that I am trying to be what I see in him. What I wanted more than before was to understand the struggle that Mr. Masterson had gone through in the early days of getting started.

That perhaps was why Mr. Masterson continually referred me to the Word of God that had been left in the office when he retired. Not sure but thankful that it was there I remembered that it was needed daily, at least I thought so, because of the peace I felt after reading something there. A past concept was when I read that God spoke to Moses and remembered that Moses heard Him say "I Am Jehovah." I needed to get deeper into understanding of that concept.

Deeper in the same area was the concept that was being explained that God was related to more than one person of time or place and that I began to wonder about the relationship that Peter and Bob had as well as Mr. Jason and his administrative assistant, Sue?

Why think about that? What part of any of the process of ABC in NY did I need to look deeper into? ABC—and then I thought about A being number one and C being number three and so I called legal on the intercom an asked, "Is there anything about ABC that we have forgotten?" Whoever was there answered and said "Boss, we will get back to you by Monday on that, OK?" Remembering that I and they were somewhere close to the same thinking I said, "Thank You."

Thinking more now about spring which was beginning to reveal itself, and the light of day getting longer, I noticed on my walk home that day that some of life was stronger. I used the cell telephone to call my wife and ask her to go to supper and get out of the apartment. She said yes.

"What was your day like?" she asked. I said "mountain climbing." Not sure about all the details of it, but I wanted to reflect that being in the office after only about a year was difficult at best. My image or thinking of Mr. Masterson's image there was different than expected I guess. She said, "Look at God and the Word." Again, here I go thinking, that's now what I wanted too here.

Speaking softly to her while we were eating I said, "pray for me." She said, "I do." Time, the staff, and the climb up the mountain with ABC is what I meant. Bringing an image of God's Word into this process and wanting to balance the understanding of the truth. The word of God identified as each part of the process.

My mind started drifting again. How old am I? When did I start this job? When did I? Where is Mr. Masterson?

Carol brought me back to the time of our being together when the song "Fascination" was playing on the system. She smiled and said remember?

Thinking back, I did remember that date, that time, but even now, it seemed like it was beyond remembering with the pressures of my life.

Remembering the "ABC" we had agreed to use "Always Be Concerned Wisely" By adding an extra letter to the ABC we had accepted a concept that ABC would become "ABCW" To me that was putting the WORD back into the concept of ABC. Mr. Masterson's place was part of my consideration.

Ignore Help Without a Plan

Give or take a few minutes it was after 10:00 pm when the telephone rang and Carol handed it to me with a strange look. "Jim, this is John. Wanted to have you hear this first from me. Tuesday you will get a call from them asking you to hold off until later and they will get back with you. They will also send a check which will amaze you. Do not let it concern you. Good night." The telephone went dead.

Mr. Masterson calling me at home with that message? Why? What had happened? Suddenly it seemed like Tuesday was a long way away and also I wanted to go climb the mountain. What a way to spend the holiday weekend. Carol looked at me and said "Can I pray?" I said not to be concerned with it, because it was normal business in our type of work. Where was the peaceful stop or part of the mountain now?

Tuesday came and I hurried to the office. The staff was all there, and looking busy, they saw me ignore the paper, the coffee and move around the telephone. The intercom did ring and the office said you have a call on line 4. Mr. Jason was quick to say "I apologize, but our two have to be on the first flight back to NY. We are shutting down the project until further notice. We are sending you a check for the progress thus far and will send you a formal letter tomorrow. Thanks and pray for our team."

That was the call Mr. Masterson had said I would get and the problem was it came for me even too quickly. Why, What, When? Was it something that I missed?

Once again the intercom buzzer startled me and I was told that there was another business on that line that wanted to speak to us. I said line 4? "Yes" Carol said. Now what?

Lead me, O LORD, in thy righteousness because of mine enemies; make thy way straight before my face. Psalms 5:8 suddenly came to me. Was there a reason this scripture or was it me learning to remember the study to show myself approved stuff? In either case I picked up the line and pushed the button for line four.

This is Mr. Sherman of the Mountain plant; how can I help you climb your mountain? I heard the words "Wow. That is a cool way to say hello. I am related to a company that I used to work for in NY and I heard that they might be coming to work on the mountain. What I wanted to do is come to work for you and I heard that you had a position open in your shipping department. It's not about the money so much, because I am semi-retired and I can have a cut in my budget, but I want to be part of your team."

Thinking back to my leaving shipping, I thought this might be an easy solution to fixed the problem that I had caused that department. I ask for their name. "Oh sorry, I forgot to introduce myself, I am Robert Jones, Retired Air Force and retired busy man. I need something to keep me inside of thinking and outside of lazy. Will you give me the chance?"

Mr. Jones send us a personal type form with your information and remember we are a business sensitive type company that handles different types of products and services, today we might be doing dog food and tomorrow missiles for Uncle Sam. You are being hired over the telephone with a permanent job in shipping with a one-year service contract being sent. Give your mailing information to the office staff when I transfer you. Regards, and see you soon.

Let's see, it is Tuesday after a three-day weekend and we have shut down a very big possibility and hired one worker? What time is lunch?

Looking Around

The remainder of the week was rather quiet. As Friday was wrapping up Carol stopped by the office and ask if she could take the rest of the day off. Her friend had a doctor's appointment and she needed a driver to help. I smiled and said, "Please go with God's blessings." That was a good feeling even though it was close to quitting. Getting ready to leave the telephone rang again and I stopped without thinking and picked up. Hello?

"Jim, this is John, stop by the coffee shop on the way home and let's talk." "Yes Sir, be there in about 15 minutes."

Looking at the Mountain I could see the glimmer on some shinning rock or piece of glass that the sun had caught just right. I said, "God show me your light again today." Then I arrived at the coffee shop and Love was right where she always laid and she jumped up like a rabbit, into my arms. Wow, what a feeling of something special.

Placing her back on the ground I said "stay." She laid back down. Thinking of the expectation of her was a real lift for my spirit. Walking in to the shop I saw Mr. Masterson sitting with Carol, my wife? What now?

Carol did not smile or jump up but sat quietly with her own special way of speaking saying in a soft but quiet way "pay attention."

Mr. Masterson said "Jim, you can call me John." I said "Yes, sir" That was just part of my military background and my respect holding me there. "What's happening?" Love was excited! "Where have you been?" He settled down and asked the water to bring a cup of tea for all three of us.

Then he smiled and said, "I am glad you handled the turn around so well. That is interesting that you have such understanding for the Mountain. Its purpose is to be able to respond to the sound of the wind, and move forward when the sun is touching the service in various ways. You did a good job and that is why I called your wife to meet me here with you tonight."

He handed me an envelope and said this is 30 percent stock of "The Mountain." There is a conditional letter written that says this stock, because of the number on them, is a joining of you and I in a responsibility of purpose for the Mountain. I am now asking you to take a higher stand or climb on the mountain with me. To take a stronger step for events like ABC and place your confidence in the rulership of the seasons that this mountain will face in the future."

There was a period of silence and then Carol said, I told him you loved Genesis 1:1—In The Beginning…and that because of your continuation with that you have ask me to be with you here and I accepted that part of our commitment and our marriage. We are one in Him and the Word."

There was a few drops of water coming out of my eye and I heard the bark of Love as she elevated herself by the window. It was like she was saying, I am glad you found me. "Mr. Masterson you have our voice and confidence as two in one for the process of this beginning. I am going to climb the mountain with a newer point of understanding.

"May I ask, when did you hire Carol, the administrative assistant? She is special and I wanted to give her a raise but with reason. She needs to have some recognition and I wanted to have her position renamed to "Administration Supervisor" with a promotion of 2.5 %. I will be willing to take that out of my salary.

He said let me be there when you do it. Call your Carol and she will be my administrative assistant with a voice and my vote. Thanks. I had better go contain the walk with Love.

Wondering If

This time of the year, ending with cold but clear weather we received a call from Guam that our daughter was going to have a baby girl. So look out Guam, here Carol comes, and we got the flight for her to be there for our first granddaughter. Back to the being left alone, staying busy, and thinking about stuff, yet I was very close to a mountain. The paper in the gift sack was very clearly protected with an official envelop.

Should I open it or wait for Carol to come back from Guam? What to do? The surprise was self-sufficient. When I got the call and John asked me if I understood why the wording of the document was such? I said "I do not clearly understand, however, trust you to do what is correct. If both your stock and ours is required before any vote is made for the company we are always voting at 55% and control the vote. That is acceptable to me."

Then the intercom buzzed and Carol said "Robert Jones is here." O.K. Thanks send him in. Mr. Jones, smiling as he entered the office said, "I have filled out all the required paper work, and with my military background do not have a problem thinking it will pass quickly. Show me my work space."

Escorting Robert to the shipping department I ask Larry to brief him and walk him through the building and introduce him. Working today, yes, but take him first to the "Loft" and get him a single for 90 days at our expense and make sure he knows where the coffee shop is.

"What a day that will be…"came flooding into my mind. What a day that would be. The mountain, the stock options of understanding, the total effort, and the addition of a person filling the job I started with. All on the same day of working without a "master plan" and yet knowing that God was watching each step.

Now and then my thinking shifted back to ABC but did not linger there too long. It was time for me to do a walk through and I started with Legal. "How are we doing? What are the highest or most important issues to get settled before the end of the year? Who wants a one week paid vacation?" Something happened in legal that day. The smiles were all around.

Moving across the hall, to Sales. Then to Networks, Financial and Shipping and then walking back to the front office or administration. Six different work areas, still in some ways separated and yet looking for more I saw something differently.

Speaking with one of the administration employees I said, which department gets the best or the most mail? Legal or Networks? Financial or Shipping, Sale's or Administration? Not including junk mail, but business mail that helps us earn our way up the mountain? He looked at me and frowned. Huh? Let me know after one month the answer to my question. Pair them off alphabetical and count the non-junk mail. Write me a short note or email the information to Carol.

The weather was changing and looked encouraging towards an early spring. Oh yes the entire staff was going to find a new way to climb the mountain. There was going to be a reason, a schedule, and a numerical pattern that could be charted for the internet publications to show. We were on the way into a different approach.

Calling shipping I ask for Mr. Jones to be sent up to the office. I said "Do you have a favorite Scripture?" Think not that I am come to destroy the law, or the prophets: I am not come to destroy, but to fulfill. Matthew 5:17 was his answer. I was amazed that he answered so quickly and very positively. "That is quiet a place to live you picked. Can I stay longer?" I said "that is the place I leased before my wife came to the mountain."

"What a day that will be..."rushed back into my mind. What a day that would be.

Working

John from Love, came the words that I remembered before. That first day, in this office, those words were strongly present in my thinking and I could almost hear, once again, the whine that Love made the day I found her on the mountain. The first day of touching her and my life with her. This force was so strong that I almost did not hear the knock on the door. Carol said, "How is your wife doing in Guam?"

I did not know because of the long distance of communication and the time difference. I said "not sure because we still do not have any communication with each other. What is the number one thing on the calendar for today?"

Carol said the requested information from the departments was on my desk and the interest level for getting something new started seemed to be central in all of their replies. What did I do to get that much going? Not sure I thought that. I wanted to ask another question, but did not do so. "Thanks, I will get started on stuff."

Thinking ahead and working without the previous financial documents, I began to wonder just what we could do in the next financial year that would put us on the plus side of the market. What makes people and or businesses find us in the yellow pages or on the internet and choose what they see for us to be part of them? The first document I looked at was from Networks. They wanted to link the entire building to the same network and work stations all with user id and login security that would document our approach. Sounded good, but what were we doing? I buzzed the intercom and ask a representative to come to the front office.

Mr. Johnson arrived and said "Boss, we are able to convert the up-to-date changes in about two weeks with a minimum cost if we choose a reliable company for service." "I said what can they learn, or take from our communications network?" "He said, boss, we will get back to you."

Then I noticed finance and their request for more paper, log pads, pens, and ink. Welcome to the real world, was my first thought. I buzzed their intercom number and said "someone come to the front office and bring a pad, if you have one." When Mr. Johnson arrived back he said, "Boss I am sorry but I work in both branches on even numbered days. Because I was made to do so a couple of years ago. What is up? Our need for paper, ink etc. will be reduced when we get into the computer network. Does that help?"

Thanking Mr. Johnson, I said, "stay in the team work thinking but let finance do their own work and you stay in networks."

I needed to find Love and pet the dog. At that moment I wanted to have my very own dog in the office, but I wanted a dog, so big and strong and so mean that they would all be afraid to come into the office. Perhaps I had better schedule a new and more frequent climb on the mountain.

I thought I should call my daughter on Guam and see what was going on. I wanted to call but did not do so at that moment because I was truly upset. Not wanting to pass it on to the expecting mother and my wife I just moved to the window and looked at the mountain. Honestly I thought I saw Love moving at the first stop level.

Making a mistake within would certainly force the incorrect tool and force the outer look of people in the internet and the yellow pages to wonder. Thinking out loud, I said "Carol—get a professional internet business contact for me on the telephone please."

Within a few minutes the intercom buzzed and she said "Internet call." I picked up the telephone and Mr. Jason said "Hello Mr. Sherman, welcome to our world! We are on the internet live and are talking to you from our Texas office, what do you want?"

Suddenly I wanted to know how to spell the word "HELP", but wanted to say, I have some questions for tomorrow and I know your end can handle the issues. Was that part of ABC coming?

The Office Staff

Getting closer to the center of newness, I asked the office staff to take a crowded seat inside my office on the next day. Doing so without permission or previously thinking about how or why, I told them I was promoting Carol to Administrative Assistant Supervisor. She would be my right and left hand in all issues. It was for her to choose how they worked as a team to better lift the burden and office toward the top of the mountain.

Each of them had been approved for their free day off on their birthday or the Monday or Friday close to it when it fell on a Saturday or Sunday, or Holiday. The next step was to ask them for the difficulty of knowing how to present a positive thought to anyone on the other end of a telephone call. If the call was within the building, or coming from outside the building, I wanted the caller to feel like they were standing on the mountain top looking down at the "Kingdom of the World." I reminded them I had read Matthew 24:14 this morning and wanted it to become part of our thinking. Thinking ahead they were at the front door of what people saw when they came into the beginning of "The Mountain."

Coordinates appointments; arranges meetings; assists with special events; provides information, including policies and procedures; may supervise, oversee activities, and or prepare schedules for staff.

Keeping the clock ticking in such a way that time was always able to be measured as interesting as well as manageable. Both were key to the lock of "The Mountain." They were considered to be by me the important part of successful business.

Wanting to expand their thinking, I asked each of them to consider promotions into the existing branches of our plant. In their estimation, I wanted to know if that could happen in a timely manner.

Having a new employee at the shipping department, as the example, reminding them that Mr. Jones was hired as my slot basic replacement and at the time he did not know that I as the leader or president of "The Mountain" used to work in the job he wanted to get hired into.

Time off, or unscheduled as required would need a supporting document, such as a Doctor's appointment and or legal issues. Advice from our own staff people was also available if they could help.

Thinking ahead, I asked for consideration of my position. The box on the wall that had been placed there was their tool to use to help me improve myself and "The Mountain."

Thanking them I ask them to pray for me and asked Carol to stay. They left and seemed to be different employees.

Carol said "Yes Sir" "What's the next ball, that you want to bounce?" I said: "Research the connection that ABC and Mr. Jason have with anything that is higher up the mountain. Research it with your touch and see if you can ring the bell that started ABC. Legal has not completely found the answer that I am looking for and I do not want them to be alarmed about the why!"

She left the office and I walked to the window. Looking at the mountain from this view I still noticed that the bible seemed to be more visible then I remembered.

Then shalt thou enquire, and make search, and ask diligently; and, behold, if it be truth, and the thing certain, that such abomination is wrought among you; Deuteronomy 13:14 was at my finger tip and I did not even understand that. I was still amazed at the power of the words in Genesis 1:1 "In The Beginning."

My thinking went to the mountain and finding Love the first day. As I was there picking the thorn from her foot and loving her I had lost myself there when the telephone intercom buzzer went off and Carol said, "It's your wife. Guam." My Carol said: "Hon, we are grandparents of a baby girl! Her name is…" the call was disconnected for some reason and I found myself crying in the stiff chair behind a very big desk, and wanting to climb a mountain that was visible outside the window.

Seven and Twelve

There was something about the number seven as well as the number twelve that troubled my thinking. The seven wings in the building and the 12 minutes it took me to walk quickly from the apartment to the office. Something kept my concern alive and it was occasionally interrupted by the sight of Love when she was present at the coffee shop.

The communication of my thoughts had to do with what month it was, or why the month was important, because our calendar had twelve of them, but we had seven different wings in the building. When I said wings, I did mean branch functions that all could be formed into one twelve function division of time and energy.

Observation of the past functions, and or, events of the building, and the business from its start which was almost exactly twelve years before. Perhaps that is why this generational thinking was going on. Remembering some of the scripture, I was reminded that there were many places when the book had statements like "the LORD came to" and things like that proved something was correct in my goal as long as it was based on the LORD.

What came to pass? When did something important or something significant happen? What calendar of events did we have to observe? Did we always do what was done in the previous event of remembering?

Going from the starting date of "The Mountain" to the current date and the events in between were relatively easy if we looked at the high and the low of each year. I did not want to find any strangers in the cycle of time and I knew, or felt strongly, that the law of the concept should be based scripturally and not financially. Getting the idea that hit my thinking I ask myself the question: Do we tithe our business, or time, our concept of the "Mountain?"

Forcing tithing into existence would be a real storm builder. Placing the concept into existence would also be, especially if at work, knowing that the employees did not accept the concept. The Mass series movies came into my thinking for some reason as I walked toward the window and looked at the mountain.

Then the idea came to me. Have each branch tithe 10% of the total reason the branch is in existence and if possible attach a scripture to the concept. What if the plan or concept would be written into the existence and if possible, do it. I wanted to say, my office, the boss office, would give 10% of my daily time to any employee who had an approved departure. Of course it would be documented and or approved for others to see as well as the legal team.

The Word? Not exactly but, I wanted to use Mark 12:9. What shall therefore the Lord of the vineyard do, he will come and destroy the husbandmen, and will give the vineyard unto others. Not truly committed to the scripture. Hebrews 13:6. So that we may boldly say, the Lord is my helper, and I will not fear what man shall do unto me. That scripture fills in a little bit better.

I was reminded that "The Mountain" did not say, or stay, alone un-thought of. It was visible in the best and the worst of weather conditions. Then it came to my mind that when the LORD spoke, sometimes the word that was said was not always obeyed.

The knowledge that the employee would like a sign or significant proof of the Word and its purpose would be necessary to understand the 10% giving concept. The idea was to prove both in Time, Truth, and Love, all the Word is necessary.

The Seven branch building can become twelve different events—monthly and or yearly—changes that will see "the Mountain" more beautiful. More powerful. More meaningful.

Intimacy

When you approach the mountain from an outsider's point of view you might consider one of four ways to get the job done. Getting the job done was what I thought was part of leadership on the Mountain.

Approaching the mountain, but unable to ascend, is a point of view found in scripture Exodus 19:11-12. Having an intimate vision of God, or your view of the mountain, but that's all you have is also found in Exodus 24:9-11. The third idea is progressing on the mountain or proceeding halfway up the mountain with Exodus 24:13-14. In view and of course there is my favorite place that I went to in the time of my hunt for the TRUTH and understanding Love before I found her there on the mountain. The scripture that supports that thinking is Exodus 33:11.

God has revealed this to me in a form of intimacy that I hardly knew existed. Reviewing a book by Chuck and Nancy Missler called "Faith in the Night Season," I realized that there is more to the concept of boss than just four letters.

So how do you get intimacy without being bossy and also get intimacy without finding fault with every mistake or malfunction? That could be the assignment given to the entire group without a day off.

Going back to when my replacement was hired for shipping and the way that it came into existence was sticking in me. Why? There is something also known as the "leadership of the Spirit" that I must learn to follow.

What do I have with my wife? What I had for the dog that was injured that day on the mountain or what I have now for "The Mountain." The question is how, when, why, or where do you stay "In The Beginning" and do not ever lose sight of God's Word in the now of that moment of need.

There are many different ways, as an example, that I can approach this matter with the different branch leadership. Asking legal to define a "legal" approach to a decision that is necessary or asking sales to make up a new idea of selling a point of interest to the mountain staff, as well as to the local community. Legal was another idea, because they always seem to be "legal" in their thinking and I still struggled with asking them to "Tell Me The Truth."

Shipping on the other hand was more or less a place of being somewhat familiar because I was employed to work there and I left there for this position of leadership. I had a handle on putting someone into that place and knew him because of the reason placed on me to choose. Administration or front office was not so easy either, because I had an office there and my senior administrative person, trusted and loved for her ability, was there, a staff of ones looking for a better way of relating were part of the new team concept.

Why did I still wonder about the empty wing? That is, we used it once in a while for conferences and things, but for the most part the hallway was dark and the office space that was supposed to be by ABC was still empty.

Looking out the window of the office, and seeing the bible on the book shelf, I saw the necessity to climb, to read, and to want to know more about the opening text "In The Beginning..."

Limited by the view of distance to the mountain, and limited by the ability to quickly climb that mountain, my thinking was still in many ways trapped by the fact, that on one climb I found a dog that I named Love, who in reality was owned by the founder of the company and he had also accepted the dog with the name. Given to him in love by a wife who has since passed away and now was in eternity.

Now the time was beginning to be more toward the concept of eternal, rather than today, or tomorrow.

Spring has Sprung

How important is the season of time related to the individual? It can be misapplied by something known as the calendar, but today was definitely a first day of spring for me. As I stepped out of the house, knowing that I was a granddad, my wife was safe, and that the "Mountain" was visible to the internet world as well as the car driving down the street, pleased my thinking, and even though I noticed Love was at her location, I was more pleased that the day had begun and that time was God's purpose for our life.

Upgrading the building to current status with all the branches internet connected to the same server and storage of data, plus links to historical access web sites and information at my location, put a bounce in my step.

Knowing that ABC had indicated by letter that the approach to trying a new idea was still on a surface burner to them and that they strongly had committed to the "Mountain" and to the idea that ABCW was still very much an issue for consideration.

Today was staff rotation and or replace someone day at the office and as I entered, I was told by security that I might get my old job back in shipping because the branch chief had called in sick "again." Now what? I took a quick look at the office paper work and told Carol that I was spending part of my day in shipping and she could contact me there if required.

Walking the hallway back towards that door was interesting in both my thinking and my concern for the supervisor. He seemed to be having more unrest, and appeared to be more unsettled. Walking in I saw Mr. Jones. "Hi there, what's up doc?" He tossed a box at me and said. I have completed the request for multiple assignable boxes for shipments and we are now able to switch on the line at four different points. We can do as few as necessary and as many as a maximum setting is required. All of that has been accomplished.

The branch chief is absent again. Starting with the line up, I asked the question: Do you want to act as lead for today? Today is the day we are all supposed to change places." He said "Yes Sir I will."

I said "OK, boss man call, me on the intercom if the line needs to run. I will be back."

Going back to the office I asked Carol for a check on the leave slip our manager in shipping had submitted. "Sick" is what it says. Speaking to her, I said "follow up with a telephone call and see if you can get the problem narrowed down."

Back to the office and the window. The Bible was still opened to the book of Exodus. The LORD is my strength and song, and he is become my salvation: he is my God, and I will prepare him a habitation; my father's God, and I will exalt him. Exodus 15:2 said: The LORD is a man of war: the LORD is his name. Exodus 15:3

Each day, in many different ways, I was able to glean on the fact that the Word of God always had a place for the immediate need. I purposed in my heart to get a handle on the leadership of our shipping branch and study it out.

Within the purpose was what could be done. What should be done? What and how did the scripture apply to the resolution of this issue. Calling back to the shipping department on the intercom, I asked the existing lead to make a comment about what he had seen since he had been hired. Was there anything that was meaningful, and if so, was it or could it be connected to a health issue for the branch chief? Do we have something inside the system that perhaps may be contributing to our employees and or the building air circulation system? Do we have a health issue that has thus been undetermined? Now that made me feel a little better, at least in part. I had accomplished something that was balanced by my idea of "In The Beginning..."

Genesis Impact

In the beginning of each moment there is something that seems to be missing when one does not consider the moment before. When I look at the mountain from the step of our apartment area, or when I look at it from the office window, especially if I am pressured by a decision making need, I sometimes forget the moment before.

The time from before I arrived at the mountain, until the time of just now, is impacted in many different ways by the moment before. As thought would have consideration, I wondered just how long Love had been held as a captured animal on the mountain, before God allowed me to climb and be the beginning of that moment of relationship.

There are so many truths that are noted by great people who have studied the book of Genesis in the time of their life and I am not troubled perhaps, but stand amazed, at the first of the book and its first three words: "In The Beginning." Because of my background I see the love of the 14 letters in the three words and the three words that make up the 14 letters are so much a part of my day's need.

The telephone interrupted my thinking as it does some times. I waited for Carol to pick up the line, but it rang a third time, and a fourth time, so I picked it up. "Welcome to the Mountain, how can we help you climb?" The telephone was silent then the branch chief from shipping said: "Boss I have some bad news: My wife has cancer. Can I get some time off?" Thinking about my wife's issue and my own issue with cancer in our lives I said "Yes, please take a couple of days now and then call me again." No comment, just silence, then he hung up the telephone.

Immediately I went to the window to look at the mountain. I remembered that 10 times in the first chapter of Genesis the words "God said" were part of verses. I wondered why I did not think of how or what God through Jesus would have said to our shipping supervisor. Why did I not know or why did I not say something better?

The beginning of this time was not just a first time, never happened before time event. Others had been through this type of event or issue. Both my wife and I had, as for understanding, been there and done that. The details perhaps were not important enough to share with him over the telephone but I wanted to have time to help him understand that God is not a respecter of persons and does not favor this one over that one even when it comes to cancer.

The intercom buzzer went off very loud so it seemed and I jumped. It was shipping saying that the product line had jammed and they were going to get behind in shipping the current product load today. Did we want to notify the client? Speaking quickly, I said to fix the problem on the equipment and if it was longer than 2 hours, to call the client and ask permission for our cost to elevate the shipment to express mail the next day. "In the Beginning God Created the Heavens and the Earth" Ten words and a total of time. Forty-Five letters put in place, in a book that governed life with or without my permission. What power was I searching for now? Certainly it was not a scripture on the "last days."

Moving into reality, now was a new beginning in a way I had not experienced before. I asked Carol to come into the office and as she did I asked her to close the door. Please help me pray that what is happening today is part of God's plan and that we at the "Mountain" will climb through the difficulty with God's Love.

She started to leave and I asked her if she knew of a good bible believing church in the city? If so, get me the pastors name and telephone number. Also to help contact the Doctors office that was handling the problem for our shift leadership. Now our department was back to three.

Without a doubt, the next day of any week time is something that needs to be correctly evaluated without fear. Walking a correct path, and being relative to fact and not fiction. Knowing the truth. The middle of time and love, truth for any or all moments. Why then do I always wonder?

Trying to communicate with my Carol on Guam after several attempts frustrated me and that was the truth. Not understanding time difference, the life of a new baby in that perspective, and the distance of what time was doing to a new love being expressed. That was reality of time. The quick interrupt of a business frustration and the expectation of "what did I do"?

Now then having a different approach to the wonder I did not realize Love was at the front door. Then suddenly I heard the bark that I had wanted to hear so many times before. She was at the door and she was talking to me.

Outside, I opened the door and she jumped into the walkway of the office as if to say, "It is about time." "Where is your daddy?" I asked. She wiggled and got down from my grip and headed toward the office window. Standing at the edge looking up and scratching, it was like she said "Mountain."

Telling Carol to cover the possibilities of the problems in shipping I left with Love and she ran towards the mountain, stopping to look back to insure that I was following her. She seemed to know why, when, and where to go. She acted like she had read the book of Genesis and wanted to get directly into the book of Exodus and that was life.

A New Storm

Without knowing for sure why, following Love to the beginning point of the mountain climb that was placed by the city for the tourist, I began to follow Love upward. Once again she only paused to see or look back. Without stopping she kept walking and sometimes even running to the next, what would appear to be, difficult stopping point. Lest I forget I had been on this mountain, and on these pathways before.

Thinking I would get to the place where I found her the first time, at the turning point where the choice was left or right she went towards the left. I had not been there that I remembered. Still not stopping she kept climbing higher. Wondering why I called her name, she stopped, came back to me, and looked straight up. I said "daddy" to her and she did not even wiggle. I said "dad" and she just looked at me.

Placing her down, at my feet, she immediately started her run walk ahead of me, looking back towards me quite often. Then I looked ahead at the slope that was there. Mr. Masterson was standing there, looking at me with a smile. "Hi Jim, she did what I asked her to do. What do you see?"

Looking towards the eastern sky then towards the western sky I said, "I see what looks like a storm coming." He said, "You're right and I wanted you to see it from here. I sent Love to you for this purpose. Please take time to tell me if you know of scripture that speaks about the storm."

For thou hast been a strength to the poor, a strength to the needy in his distress, a refuge from the storm, a shadow from the heat, when the blast of the terrible ones is as a storm against the wall. Isaiah 25:4 was the scripture he mentioned to me. Obviously I did not know it.

Hearing that from him was an eye opener as far as storms coming. I wanted to know more about what he was thinking in terms of the overall status of "The Mountain." He told me that I should give consideration to Mr. Jackson, from Shipping, because of the medical problem a year on paid, administrative leave with the option to work some hours at night as a security guard. That would keep him in touch, but take some of the pressure off of the medical issues.

Then he said something that surprise me. "This is your decision, not mine." Hearing that caused me to look again at the storm that was on the horizon. He said "Jim, decisions can be sometimes difficult to make, but they should always be lined out with the scripture."

Starting down the path away from the visual stand of watching the storm approach, he said "Let's go get a cup of coffee, call the office, and let staff go home early because of this storm and ask them to come in earlier tomorrow." What a climb.

A distant clap of thunder, and an extreme bolt of lightning, appeared at the edge of the storm. The voice I heard was distant yet clear. "Listen to my word. Listen to it and accomplish it through my visibility." I looked at Mr. Masterson and said "What"? He smiled and said "the climb down is always easier than the climb up."

Distant thunder again. Walking with him, and being visible within his step was so refreshing that I almost forgot to look at Love. She was leading both of us down the mountain and seemed to want to be casual about that.

Within the hour of our visit it started raining and the wind settled into a strong storm wind. The path had been changed in visibility, and the desire to get more of God's Word deeper into my spirit was very strong. Back to the chapters in Exodus.

And Moses cried unto the LORD, saying, what shall I do unto this people? They are almost ready to stone me. Exodus 17:4 Why that scripture when I looked at the book again. The bible was fun but sometimes difficult to read and understand.

Nowhere or Somewhere - That is the Question

Unsettled in the thought of now, or the thought of tomorrow, is not uncommon with me. The meeting with Mr. Masterson, his knowledge of what was inside the plant, and the status of the supervisor of shipping. All of that and the wonder of what he was thinking about me. Here by his choice, walked from a third position place in shipping to an empty front office with a window, a visible outlook, and a bible. He knew all of that and he knew Carol. My thinking was I am nowhere and yet I am somewhere. The question for me is why do I think that way?

The time of the visit with Mr. Masterson, was a needed time. Feeling somewhat different, I thought that I knew some things rather well. As an example, looking at the financial paperwork, or looking at the status of a job in progress, or looking at the out flow of the product during shipping. They all seemed like a good thing, yet for some reason, they appeared to have little value if I was standing in the presence of Mr. Masterson. Doubtfully thinking it was not Love that helped me feel incorrectly either.

My expectation for the call expected from NY came at that moment. I was bouncing up and down when I heard the intercom announcement for the call. NY on line one. "Yes Sir, what are the target dates for the project?" A period short as it was, of silence, and then Mr. Jason said "Glad you're so aggressive, towards the project. Let me have you sit down."

"The first thing is to let you know that you and yours passed the test of initial interest in "The Mountain." We are sending you a document that will help explain what is next. Please read it carefully and review it for timing and contextual setting. We want to get off to a great start at the first of the year." With that comment, he hung up the telephone. I sat amazed at a nothing telephone call that was either No Where or Some Where and that was my question. Where, What, When, Why, and more than that, Help Me LORD.

Carol told me that my wife had called from Guam and that she would be coming at the end of the week back to the states. We would have lots of pictures to look at and perhaps a new thing to talk about when she arrived.

The intercom buzzed again and Carol said it was Mr. Jackson from shipping. He asked me how things were going at the plant and wanted to know if he could work as security guard on Tuesdays and Thursday and perhaps Saturday and or holidays. I advised him that his position was secure and that the days for that would be alright. Only call the security branch chief to let them know, and they could communicate with the front office on any changes to that schedule that might be required.

The intercom buzzed again and this time it was sales. "Guess what boss, we just got a huge job offer worth significant financial increases. You many need to hire some more people. Will give you the details at the weekly meeting."

No Where or Some Where at the same time. Thinking about the mountain talk with Mr. Masterson, and the need for prayer, I went to the window and looked at the mountain. I could not clearly say anything that seemed to make sense of what was going on. Then I thought about what Mr. Jackson had said, what Mr. Masterson had said, and what the clouds looked like hanging over the mountain top and I said. "God, I love the visibility of your word alive in the time and place of your Mountain. Bless it with your love and help me to know your step. Thank You Lord."

Thinking about Carol coming home and the apartment's need for her return in a couple of days, I thought I had better go get some food.

Climbing the Mountain

When the weather changes, and the day seems different, the pressure of a decision at work and the relationship these things might have within me makes me wonder. Thinking of this, I have learned to look at the bible differently, not just a denominational church way of thinking "the bible says" but asking God to help me with the moment in time when I feel like leaving the work building and or the problem and climbing.

Then Moses climbed the mountain to appear before God. The LORD called to him from the mountain and said, "Give these instructions to the family of Jacob; announce it to the descendants of Israel: Numbers 19:3

Now if you will obey me and keep my covenant, you will be my own special treasure from among all the peoples on earth; for all the earth belongs to me. Numbers 19:5

So easy to find or look at and yet at times so easily forgotten to do first. Waiting until the last moment is not my exact life style. In fact, getting ahead of the next event is usually what I do, but, I have learned that it is now always wise. The first things first attitude is not really stuck within me so that it becomes a stronger force.

When I first arrived here, there was no doubt that I wondered about the mountain, from a long way away. I saw it first on the horizon, then the next time I reflected of course it was taller and closer and more visible. Still I did not honestly get it. The visual part of it from a distance, versus, a visual part of it standing at the bottom, just before being able to climb.

Exodus 19:11 Be sure they are ready on the third day, for on that day the LORD will come down on Mount Sinai as all the people watch. You might say, oh, that is just another verse in the book. But, why did God allow it to be a part of my life so quickly now? Another step up the mountain. Why? When do you want to know more about the very next step in your process?

Exodus 19:17 Moses led them out from the camp to meet with God, and they stood at the foot of the mountain. Provable that leadership to or toward God is visible and it is necessary. The leadership of today, versus what I knew or thought I knew, yesterday or a week ago, or even before I walked from the shipping room to the front office. Each day was part of God.

Exodus 19:25 So Moses went down to the people and told them what the LORD had said. In other words, there is more to the moment of each day, than just a verse or two, here and there. My wife was coming home and I had heard that speaking from her lips, but I truly ignored it many times over. Now I think I understood a little better why the Lord allowed us to be separated by even such as a grandchild being born several thousand miles away. How tall is this mountain, that God has placed me near? Why does it seem so easy to see and difficult to climb?

188

The purpose then, to wonder about the climb on the mountain, has been anchored into my spirit and the voice of the Lord's word has to be what I use to measure the steps that I take. Each day to and from, or looking at, the mountain could be measured by the idea that God is watching the mountain and it is nearer my life.

Picking up my wife that night was a mixed set of emotions. Wanting her home, yet, not able to confess that I needed more of God's Word in me thinking each day. Having her so closely visible to be that tool was a wonder to me at this point in my life. The mountain was light, even at the night time hour with the airport tower lights there. Even today, I can remember that I had totally ignored that.

The trip back to the house was about Guam and the baby that was so special. Our first granddaughter and a reason to go back to Guam in our future. What was I doing on the mountain? Why did I think I was secure in a single place, with a go do it now job? What was in my thinking issue that I had totally ignored the concept of scripture that said "And he said unto them, go ye into all the world, and preach the gospel to every creature." Mark 16:15.

Steps That Matter

The next week was not troubled in ways of misunderstanding, but perhaps troubled by the steps necessary to walk correctly toward the end of the path. It reminded me of my first climb on the mountain, the days before I found Love. The days when I was searching for things to be important without a full understanding that the Word of God was what I should be understanding.

Within reason, like a change in the season of time, we expect certain things to happen just because we were told that it should. If winter did not come on December the 22nd then we perhaps we would ask when it was scheduled. My concern had to deal with the call from NY about the "Mountain" being part of the plan.

That concern was answered. Mr. Jason called me at 8:00 a.m. The call was unexpected but welcomed because I needed to have more definite steps in my experience. It was easy for me to want Mr. Masterson to fix the problem. It was easy for me to make or think about the factual steps to take in business. However, the steps for the future, and the magnitude of such steps was a burden.

Mr. Jason said that "The Mountain" had won the idea contest or contract and that ABC in NY would be making us a branch of them. We would be known as ABCW, or Always Be Concerned Wisely." ABC would underwrite our existence in the new concept. Our business would be to be available to contract truckers when they needed us to handle their load for overnight shipping. That did not sound difficult, but I wondered about what trucks, and how many, and when they would be parking in our area.

Immediately Mr. Jason said, not to worry about the details because a team of five would be on the airplane tomorrow to step up the contacts and the understanding of core that would be accomplished in this part of our business. We would still be known as "The Mountain" but would have the ABCW wing as a growth part of the new concept. Mr. Jason said he and Mr. Masterson had been personal friends for years and they stood together in this new look. Our business was about to expand from a regional area business to a statewide, country wide business with a name that would be respected.

What could I say now? The time had changed for me to get a deeper look at the power of God's Word and understanding the truth. Even in the 19th chapter of Exodus where the 10 commandments were laid out there was structure and reason. Mr. Jason ended his call with a "Welcome to ABC" and as "Part of the Team, I would be getting a significant raise." My concept was to wonder? Why me Lord? What are you planning for my walk in my relationship with you?

Calling Carol at home, I told her that we might be moving into something, somewhere a little different and perhaps bigger. Our future was and is being changed by God's Love. Then I could not help but remember the time when I found the dog, on the mountain and needed it. "Love" even before I knew that it was the dog that belonged to Mr. Masterson, and that his wife had named the dog.

There was and is a pattern in this concept, and I had not until now realized that the Word of God follows the same truth. If one does look at it, or should I say, study it, then the concept of the 10 commandments in Exodus is not difficult to understand. Perhaps wondering about the book of Revelations is still within reason.

Wanting to stay on the "Mountain" was not necessarily just a bigger pay job concept, but rather seemed to be a realization the bible, in the book holder, under the window where one could see the mountain on a day of personal desire was a good thing.

Thinking about tomorrow and getting up to speed on the new function of the 8th wing of our building would be interesting. Asking Carol to schedule an immediate staff meeting with key staffers from each wing was fun to do. "Let me tell you about ABC and ABCW."

Now We Are One

The ABC team arrived as previously announced and walked in on a Thursday morning all smiles. Saying the focus would be a one-day event, could they be assigned or could they choose their places. Saying you choose, one said, "I will do legal", another said "sales" a third said "contractors", a fourth said "networks" and the last said "as usual I get stuck with financial." As they departed they turned and said we will meet you in shipping at 10:30.

As expected the 10:30 time happened quickly. They all gathered there with me in shipping and said this is the new center. We as ABC will build a new wing, here with two loading or processing locations. The largest road truck will be comfortable here. We will also build a sleep center for the drivers should they stay during the process of re-cycling the loads. It should never take more than 24 hours at any given day. By the way, remember this new wing will be open Monday through Saturday as required. Always closed on Sundays, e.g. God's Day.

Let's go back to the front office and wrap this up. Looking at my watch it was only 12:30 and we had not had or stopped for lunch. I mentioned going to the local area and their leader said, "no we have another air plane to catch at 2:30"

Back at the front office they explained that when notified, we would be told, in advance that an 18 wheeler would stop because of the need. The identified load of merchandise would be off loaded and re-loaded into our system. Our system then, would repackage the load with a new box. The box would carry the ABCW label. Each box would be processed with the shipping information change necessary to get it reassigned to the new schedule. Each box and or shipment would be processed to arrive at the designation within 24 to 48 hours from the received time. The receipting would be notified and we would be required to get it done. Any questions?

My first was for our team. They replayed that each branch had been given a work folder to accomplish the process within the allotted time. The secret to the success would always be the correct assignment of scripture to the ABCW work process. Nothing would leave the sight without a scripture. Nothing. My thinking was perhaps motivated by the time that I wanted to reclaim the "mountain."

Had I ever climbed the mountain, talking or thinking or wondering about a scripture? Now the Exodus book was heavy on my heart. They as a people were moved from captivity into freedom and they were told by God how to get it done.

Moving a little stronger into the lead, I ask permission to pray over the process before the first actual truck arrived or before this crew left. They said "Please." My prayer was simple: "In The Beginning God, Created the

Heavens and the Earth. Lord, help us climb the ABCW mountain together so that you alone would be glorified, and that the Word would be first and for most."

Thanking the guest, they departed and said quite friendly, "see you on the internet"? Then my flip flop active thinking came back. Help, Mr. Masterson.

Asking the staff to stay, I said "you all have your package, you all have an assignment of knowledge, and you now all have a job that adds this thought to your day. Any touch of your branch to this project will always be accomplished with a scripture." Prayerfully place them in a visible way on your letter head and or your documentation. Remember this singular rule. Do Not Get Stuck in a Religious Rut. The Word is alive. Remember the truth.

Jesus said to her, "I am the resurrection and the life. The one who believes in me will live, even though they die; John 11:25 My verse for today and every third Thursday would be this one at least until I climbed the mountain once again.

A new beginning with a new shipping dock and a wondering about the first call of the required new functions. Meeting with each branch chief, I was assured that they understood their responsibilities of the functions required.

For example, proper identification of the truck, the driver, the proof of insurance, and the expected documentation load in question. Given 24 hours with internet access to communicate with ABC.

Wondering just why a truck would be re-routed to our location would be tested more than once because it was scheduled by ABC to be a recurring and regular function. They had re-addressed the concept of spreading the gospel with a declaration of the truth. This was a scripture based function and not to be considered as a money making project. Each time a truck was encountered, their respect, their consideration for their job, and the delivery of a process that God has placed into existence was a very strong concept.

Mr. Masterson called, saying "Jim how goes it?" Explaining that the docks were in place, the security had been upgraded with improvements, and the crew in shipping had been expanded to include one member from each branch on any given truck day was accomplished. Waiting on the first truck. That was the difficult thing for me. He said, "This has been part of my vision for a number of years. Prayerfully, we are entering into a new and different type of work and ministry. God bless." The line went blank and a truck was still pending.

Reviewing each branch from the first to the last I was impressed with the initial scriptures they had selected. In particular, the legal team. And he said unto them, go ye into all the world, and preach the gospel to every creature. Mark 16:15. That was one that I had wanted to use.

Looking at the "yesterday" of our location I was missing something that was obviously available. We as a structured team had grown together in outreach.

Today was a day of expectation, whether that would come by telephone, internet, or email was beyond me, but I knew I wanted it to be expected and wanted.

Forever, that was truly another matter. How do you plan for that, when your struggling with both the yesterdays and the todays of your life with or without the scripture support in your thinking? Then again, I wanted to call all the department chiefs and say prayerfully think ahead for today and forever. Yesterday is a day we are thankful for.

We were encouraged by the ABC team to write personal information to be sent with the shipments when the process required the load to pass through our center. As we were located somewhat near the center of traffic and interstate highways I expected a rush on the timing of the first truck, yet it seemed delayed. Then I thought about more than just one KJV scripture. Why not tell someone where, when, or why God allowed my life to be changed.

What was or what is the reality? Without a doubt, the one thing I had against all churches and God was what I thought was the lack of reality. Maybe it was my past, and being raised in a foster farm home because my real father and mother divorced when I was three. Perhaps it was my return into a mother and step father relationship when I was nine years old, forced into a family that I did not know, and perhaps it was watching my two older brothers run away from that home two days after we were placed there together. Perhaps it was trying to learn to live with a step sister and a step brother who seem to do no wrong, while I was punished for walking into the house late, or not cleaning my room just right. Perhaps it was being non-Christian, or not saved.

Meeting Christ as I did was because I, as a young man, started playing church because mom and my step father wanted me to be there, and oh yes, while you're there stop by the corner store and pick up the paper. My life was changed as I grew older into a run from God or salvation life into a run away from home life and it was that way until the day I first saw my "girlfriend" but did not know that she was a Christian.

Then life changed. I had been in the Air Force about 3 and ½ years and I had a difficult do nothing job for the Air Force that was constantly changing. Once again I came face to face with reality but did not know that it was God who caused me to wonder about him. My testimony then was meeting Him because He wanted me to. Which steps matters? It is the first one, that a person does make, but it is hindered by a force also known as the "enemy" that wants us not to make that step.

Step #1 Remember that God is. He does watch over us.

Step #2 The Process of revealing how much HE loves us and what we do about that love.

Step #3 Begin to take one more step towards HIM because you accept by faith, you are.

Step #4 Breathing air, which HE created for you to know HIM.

Having said that I have walked according to the Word as I learned from it, and the Psalm 30:4 that says "Sing unto the LORD, O ye saints of his, and give thanks at the remembrance of HIS holiness"

There is a forever, and it is established by the fact that we have all had a past or a yesterday, and we have experienced a today. What God allows us to do for HIM in our tomorrow will be much more than just unloading a truck full of stuff and placing a note in it that says "Jesus loves you."

The first truck arrived exactly on time and Jim Johnson stepped out. Looking somewhat tired and anxious he said "Is this the Mountain Stop?" I said yes and I am also Jim. Welcome. Let's bring your documentation into legal and shipping will start the unload.

Sales will show you the rest apartment for your two or three-day stay. Contracts will have the truck relocated to service for a 100% end to end upgrade with your engine difficulty and the tire issues. Shipping will have the unload complete by the end of the day and reroute of your shipping will be handled internally. Administration is here to help with any and all of your necessary paper work. After you have had a full night's rest and a good meal, expenses paid, you might want to climb the Mountain for a while.

All of the support work is being accomplished because you are a Christian driver that has accepted the Lord and we want to be part of your life in the ABCW ministry. Always Be Concerned Wisely was a local extension of ABC in NY.

The information we had currently will indicate that your shipment load from our location will go to Alabama. From that drop off you will go to Baltimore and from there you will end going somewhere in Cleveland. That was passed to us before your arrival. In other words, you have been scheduled and you have a mission planned by ABC to further the gospel.

We have some printed publication material we will give to you when you depart. Welcome, once again, to the

Mountain. Psalms 125:2 As the mountains surround Jerusalem, So the LORD surrounds His people. From this time forth and forever. If you have any other questions and or concerns, feel free to dial the number on our business card.

When you stop for a moment and see, we are one, In Him. HE is the Reason we are alive and we are blessed because HE Lives. Think about the mountain that may be part of your life, then climb it with the WORD alive in your heart.

The Zero

On the road to recovery, the concept of the difference between zero and one struggled in my way of wonder. Why did the idea or needing to know about zero, or hoping after I learned that the part of that matters, I could or would know the value of one?

Looking at the concept of zero, Z particle as a heavy, uncharged element particle considered to transmit the weak interaction between other elementary particles. It has as, which I place as a reason of E-Eternity or an eternal lasting or existing forever, without the end or the beginning. The R value, or the capacity of an insulating material to resist heat flow. The O ring which is a casket in the form of a ring with a circular cross section, typically made of pliable material, as used to seal connection in things such as pipes, comes into what I need to know. So much for zero.

Then starting to count, I cannot find a way to do so unless I accept the concept that there was a zero number or there was nothing before the one. Did something exist? The Word of God, simply says "In The Beginning God created the Heavens and the Earth." Then I believe there was something between or provable.

Day by day, or moment by moment, which is a huge difference, illustrates what I wanted to begin with. Struggling to know the truth about everything in my walk with both the concept of the Word and the truth of the Word. The study of this word from the bible in John 8:32 says that we can know the "a-la-tha-a" as it is written in the Greek original and it will, should you or me or us, the way or the truth.

Moments from now, into a day of eternity, is the path, for what we call living, and the truth is supposed to be the heartbeat, of that walk. Forever from yesterday, or perhaps thinking of a distant tomorrow that has reason, is what the difference is because we need to know the distance between right and what is called wrong. Like the distance between the idea that zero and one does not matter, unless the test of life and death are being measured.

Then why do we wonder or care about something as simple as something like a zero? If it is in the value system of numbers, associated to the balance of a bank account it could be positive or negative depending on the location. Once I remember counting the balance of my checking account and something told me that I had zero balance. The zero balance I had was a negative value of more than 10.00 dollars. Why? When did something change?

Look at this from a different stand point. It may not be day light when you open your eyes, but, something, somehow, speaks a thought to your mind and says "do not be concerned" because there is light coming, if it is not visible now. Some assurance of time between the no light and light seems to be peaceful, because we may assume that light will be. Is that removal of the zeros in our thinking or is it a plus of something making us accept the fact that one exists, even when we cannot see the number clearly?

Then a measurement between the zero and the one is determined by factual thinking of memory into some way of existence. Within or without the time of now, there is the possibility of some interaction that will cause the negative side of zero to become a positive side, so that there can be something else to look at. One more of anything is better thinking so to speak, than some of nothing forever. Without a dog in my life in the past, my thinking would be that there was no mountain there, nor did I climb it. No friend with a name to remember. Softly and to remember that there is something worth knowing. The zero of life can be remembered as the one thing that must never leave my definition of truth. Knowing the truth as mentioned prior to this is still a way of acceptance to something else. There is proof that a zero has become a one.

There is proof that the air we breathe is there because the creation of it was proven once again. Each time you or I touch the thought process of thinking, we leave the zero in a way that one seems special. When someone said count from 1 to 10, and I was only two that seemed like a problem. Perhaps they could have said, start with a zero and work your way forward in God's love. Yes, I could not understand that at the age of two either, but there was life, both in my past having been born, and there was a future, to the now of this life. Zero no longer has a holding point. The number one, issue as is stated in the Word is "In The Beginning."

One Way

Dealing with the zero and wanting to run, or in another way of saying getting caught in a sealed way of knowing that there is more to it, I jumped at the opportunity to think about one. The word one appears 1967 times in the 1695 verses of the KJV bible. So what? The original word has to go with the idea of "Go one way or another", which is the reason I was thinking about the zero and the one.

Now that I am here, and this is a part of the book, entitled "Time, TRUTH, Love" I really want to get to the point. Time, truth, and love are the reason for this book. If you have read this far, and you understand, that several printings of multiple stages for proof reading and so forth, then you will realize that the entire book, in existence is multiplied by reason.

There is a consideration for picking on zero first. The idea in and of itself, as presented overcoming realization of how much I have need of. The fact that the number one is important, yet after the acceptance of zero, was a beginning. Throughout this book the expression "in The Beginning" has been referenced.

The fact of getting to the number or word "one" was not the original reason for the book. It is actually part of an attempt to find a way to end a book that could get hundreds of chapters or pages. It is a winter time and I need something to do.

Reaching out, or moving from zero to one, is only an example of trying to explain the process of having experienced the process of medical damage and why I can now say, I have progressed from 0 to the 1 stage.

The start of the book, or the story called or entitled the "Mountain", perhaps did not tell you enough. The introduction of Time, Truth, and Love explanation did not say what you understood. Chapter 52 perhaps will not say enough to explain what happened when the medical damage to my left brain took place. Walking, talking, and not thinking, or understanding time, truth, and love is difficult to just say "so there."

The drifting between the parts of me that made up a story or the concept of a business in a place, l and the added information of my personal life, within the pages is now part of adding something to the zero that was there, to something called truth.

Now alive in the 76-year-old body, with an 8 year and growing old or up brain, functional person is what has impacted lives of family, friends, as few as they are, and most of all my relationship with the LORD God, who provided the air that I now know He has given me to breath once again. The past of yesterday, or the looking back to a zero place in life, was accomplished in ways that perhaps were different. Others without medical reason have trouble wondering about the now in life, let alone the past, and perhaps they even struggle with the tomorrow.

"In The Beginning" of the scripture has a powerful truth associated with it. Yes, it is there, and has been more years than I can count or remember. Yet without saying "I told you so," it is more powerful than perhaps even the most difficult stranger to the book can wonder about.

When the pages of this book or writing are locked up in a printed format, will it matter? Perhaps to or for some reason, but only once in a lifetime each person has a moment in time, that you might remember, that there is one in a million like you, because we are all as it is said breathing "air." But, it is God's provision.

The struggling with a title for the book, or writing, and the effort to get to a place that has a resting point has been, and still is of saying things, like I am glad it is settling into the winter of 2015. Yes, I had a birthday, this year, and turned 76. Yes, the leaves are almost all out of or off of the trees in the yard and they do need to be cleaned up. An 8-year-old has the job, using a 76-year-old body to get the job done, but they are, excuse the pun, "trying to get the job done."

Walking through the life and the existence of "Time, Truth, and Love" is proof that in so many different ways we are in "The Beginning."

Encephalitis Information

Encephalitis = "E" Eternity or Everywhere.

Perhaps a different way of proving that time and test is still present. A new day, and a new time of that day that seemed to have passed without even being announced. That was the reason why, but not also known for sure as proof that such a day exists in time. Looking for it, from the present time is easy, when you know that you are missing something that is life changing. But, knowing that is missing, or even thinking that what you missed was important is another point in the same day.

Without the past, or the knowledge of the past, the matter of missing what is clearly absent would not necessarily be acceptable, or understood. Once the time is present to be wondered, then someone else perhaps may enter into the time. Only you in my life, plays in the back ground, and the words of the song become so necessarily real.

Being here now is part of time, and then someone with something as simple as a telephone call will interrupt that time. Giving you nothing in return except notice that their time is now your time. Endless love? Perhaps, but was it God, through the Holy Spirit that did it? Then the song, "I Only Have Eyes for You" plays and you ask why? "My One and Only Love" is the next on the I-Tunes play listed that just down loaded to the computer you are using to type this document. Now what do you think of time and love and the reasons life goes bye. Only you?

The day after tomorrow is important when you think about the fact that it is the day Uncle Sam is supposed to pay you for time past. What, why, when or where do they care and will they continue? They all will disappear to you accordingly to the song that has words that is playing in the background, and it is only because "you only have eyes."

Encephalitis = "N" Nothing or Nowhere.

The second letter of the word Encephalitis. When it started, at least from the point of remembering, the head aches were noticeable, yet ignored. Place in a period of not dealing with truth. From that point to the actual point of lost was several months, broken down into time off for abnormal behavior. Not totally noticeable by family or friends to the point of warning. The last days were me placing myself into bed without reason, and without communication to get the help needed. For the next weeks, doctors' appointments, and treatment went from nothing to wrong, to nowhere or nothing. Little guidance from the truth, the time or the love. Re-thought it could be said the Time, The TRUTH and The Love that was only measurable now, by the completion of time and the eight years of looking back.

Encephalitis = "C" Concern or Corners.

Real time getting nowhere without understanding. Actually a Doctor stopped the up side down approach and rushed me into medical treatment at a local hospital when my condition reaching a point of being close to why? What Is Encephalitis?

Encephalitis, or inflammation of the brain tissue, is rare, affecting about one in 200,000 people each year in the U.S. When it strikes, it can be very serious, causing personality changes, seizures, weakness, and other symptoms depending on the part of the brain affected. (Web MD).

Encephalitis = "E" Events or Excellence of Eternity.

Many people who have encephalitis fully recover. The most appropriate treatment and the patient's chance of recovery depend on the virus involved and the severity of the inflammation. In acute encephalitis, the infection directly affects the brain cells. In para-infectious encephalitis, the brain and spinal cord become inflamed within one to two weeks of contracting a viral or bacterial infection. Not known to family or friends in the hospital I was not able to communicate.

The medical team, first went in the incorrect path and through the hand of God's guidance arrived at the correct determination that it was a brain infection. This was completion of a spinal tap. At that time, I was completely gone from the communication state.

Encephalitis = "P." Perhaps or Prayer.

Early in the AM of that day, they put me into surgery and opened the left side of my head to remove the material that was infected by the problem of location and late understanding. In this time, I did have an escape of my reality into or what is called a dream. There are other names for it, and I can remember the parts of it now, even eight years later. But, I cannot remember the correct way to refer to a "vision" or a "miracle" if you move into the spiritual part of this medical experience. Perhaps it was or is now being answered by prayer.

Encephalitis = "H." Health or Healing.

That is not a question so much as it is a wonder of time. We now refer to things in terms that a person speaking or a person listening perhaps have different thinking about. Health is something thought of, perhaps not understood, and Healing is of course a greatly misunderstood term used by people, who try to explain away health without correctly dealing with Time, Truth, and LOVE. Encephalitis = "A" Attitude or Affection. Time is changing the way I am thinking about the past and the present. During the last two months I have written a book, as they say, called by the title given "Time, Truth, Love." Much of it was done in the personality of "Hislerim" which is my pen name. Given the fact that Encephalitis has twelve letters I still have a lot of things to write about. Encephalitis = "L" Life and Love. Both of which are part of the experience that is being dealt with now. Listening to a piece of classical music has a different meaning as well as looking out the window and having a special interest in the wind moving just one limb or leaf on the tree. That part of now is special in life and love. It is now more important to remember but difficult to establish because the left brain damage is still evident in different ways.

Encephalitis = "A" Always thinking, or trying to remember.

The idea is that it was approximately eight years ago that this even took place and the medical part or doctor's part of my life is not filling in the blank places. It is something I need to address with them. Trying to get that done.

Encephalitis = "L" Loss of Liberty.

That is the question. Who keeps me in the proper path of travel and knowledge, without a truthful understanding of the fact that I am a problem patient? There has to be moveable application to the issues that need to be dealt with.

Encephalitis = "I" Interest or Income.

That is the question. The book that I did is to me a book of interest because I needed to do it. Yes, it is written here, and I am not busy outside in my escape from reality or life, however, the book is not about the "income" of sales and the product of a completed book was honestly a challenge. To write the story, without being ridiculous about the way the professionals want you to use them and pay them was part of the interest as well as part of the income. I did not write just to make money, but I did write to help the cure of encephalitis in my interest.

Encephalitis = "T" Truth of Test.

Only time will provide the truth of the test. The Word of God has a very important way of proving what I said. "In The Beginning", the opening three words of the KJV of biblical experience, have fourteen letters broken by three portions or steps. The word "IN" is a two letter word with the letter "I" as the first part. Everyone seems to be motivated by the self or "I" complex of time. But to be "IN" the Word and "IN" a personal relationship with Christ is a different world of time. "The" as an expression of the three in one, as a three letter word that has a single meaning was in a different way difficult to talk or explain. It is just a simple word "the", but has so many difficult ways of attachment to something like the word that follows it. "Beginning" with was the nine letters of difficulty.

Looking at it from the numerical standpoint or view, it was necessary to remove the letters of duplication because of the initial exposure from the two letter word "IN" but, removing the "i's" the "n's" and the "g's" the only thing I noticed was once again the fact that only two letters "BE" were left. Be - Truth in the TEST.

Encephalitis = "I" "S" Invested of Interest.

Easily to understand, but better to deal with when the "I" is connected to the last letter of the word encephalitis. "IS" That seems to be for me at this point the time, the Truth, and the LOVE. I am sorry for the things I have done, in the old me, and the difficulty of being a truthful, totally lovable person in the part of recovery, but, still the time document I have finished is now just that. Encephalitis in reality. Time and Truth has proven God's LOVE.

About the Author

Born in Kalamazoo, Michigan July 14th 1939 my family was even then in a mountain of difficulty. My mother had been divorced because of an alcoholic relationship with my real father and he was on the road so to speak.

Struggling with life I was placed in a foster farm location with the placement more for the need than for the reality of what I knew. Dad and Mom Peas where the foster parents, having two children of their own and they were responsible for getting the job done.

Moving back into a reestablished relationship with my mother and her second husband, I graduated from high school by force so to speak when I left home at the age of 17 and joined the United States Air Force. During my tour and time met my wife in September of 1959 and was married. Thought out the time factor I stayed in the Air Force for 23 and ½ years and retired.

While looking for something to do and staying busy I re-entered the Civil Service Work Force and became another around the busy network of time until I reached 22 years of time. During this time of my life I was ordained with the Independent Assembly of God church.

James S. Sherman

Made in the USA
San Bernardino, CA
26 May 2016